MW00906760

WORLD WAR II

A SOURCE BOOK

This is a Flame Tree Book
First published in 2003

01 03 05 04 02

1 3 5 7 9 10 8 6 4 2

FLAME TREE PUBLISHING
Crabtree Hall, Crabtree Lane, Fulham,
London, SW6 6TY, United Kingdom
www.flametreepublishing.com

Flame Tree is part of
The Foundry Creative Media Company Limited

Copyright © 2003 Flame Tree Publishing

ISBN 1-904041-45-0

A copy of the CIP data for this book is available from the British Library

Printed in China

Special thanks to Sonya Newland

A SOURCE BOOK

Jon Sutherland
& Diane Canwell

Introduction by Paul Cornish

FLAME TREE
PUBLISHING

CONTENTS

Each chapter is divided into entries and organized chronologically

INTRODUCTION

The importance of the subject of this book can scarcely be over-emphasized. Unparalleled in scale by any other conflict in human history, World War II is generally estimated to have cost the lives of 50 million people. In terms of human suffering its effects are incalculable, and the physical destruction that it wrought took decades to repair. Without a full knowledge of this cataclysmic event it is impossible to understand fully the history of the second half of the twentieth century.

This was the war that propelled the USA to the status of 'Super-Power', by hugely enhancing its economy and military might. Another of the war's victors, the Soviet Union, matched American power for over 40 years, creating the Cold War. That a real war never erupted between these

antagonists was largely due to the fact that both possessed arsenals of nuclear weapons – another development of World War II. Meanwhile, with their economies shattered by the war, the traditional 'Great Powers' of western and central Europe lost much of their influence in the world. They also proved unable, through lack of economic power and political will, to hold onto their empires.

In the Middle East, the creation of the state of Israel was hastened by the arrival of Jewish survivors of Nazi persecution. Israel's aggressive defence of its independence, against attempts by neighbouring Arab states to extinguish it, resulted in recurring conflicts during the second half of the twentieth century. Its existence remains the central factor in the complicated politics of the region. Further east, China, already ravaged by civil wars, had been invaded by Japan in 1937. By 1945 its Nationalist government was so weakened and discredited that Mao Tse Tung's well-organized army was able to begin the unification of the world's largest nation under Communist rule.

The war itself exhibited many novel features. Firstly it was a global war: few regions of the world remained untouched by its effects. Furthermore, civilian populations experienced war on a wider scale than ever before. Even those fortunate enough to escape invasion, bombardment, enemy occupation or famine could be affected by the unprecedented level of mobilization on the home front or, at the very least, by shortages caused by the disruption of international trade.

World War II was also a war of conflicting political ideologies. This conflict was complicated by the fact that western democracies were obliged to make a common cause against Nazism, Fascism and Japanese Militarism with the Communist Soviet Union. The western Allies had no

◀ *LEFT: A meeting of the Allied leaders during World War II.*

territorial claims to make on their opponents; their sole aim was to destroy the enemy political regimes. The USSR had very real ambitions to expand its power, but was happy to achieve this by imposing the rule of Soviet-controlled Communist governments in countries that Soviet troops had liberated.

Many of the weapons and tactics employed in World War II originated in World War I; however, the technological advances of the intervening 20 years now allowed them to show their full devastating potential. The early German successes were built on their so-called Blitzkrieg tactics – employing massed tanks with close air support. As the war progressed, these tactics were refined and adopted by other countries too – most successfully by the USSR. Change was equally evident in naval warfare, where the rise to prominence of naval aviation ensured that the aircraft carrier replaced the battleship as the prime naval unit. Meanwhile ocean-going submarines fought major campaigns in the Atlantic and Pacific Oceans. Massed aerial bombing of enemy cities

◀ *LEFT: Preparations for the First Battle of El Alamein in 1942.*

was pioneered by the Germans, but brought to a terrifying peak of efficiency by the British and Americans against Germany, and the Americans against Japan. The latter campaign culminated in the deployment of a wholly new type of weapon – the atomic bombs.

All these aspects of World War II are clearly and concisely presented to the reader of this book. Descriptions of the events and campaigns appear in chronological order, along with the political background from which they sprang. Interspersed within this structure are discussions of the tactics and weapons used. The book is further enlivened by the inclusion of biographies of the leading political and military figures of the era. Full advantage is taken of the ready availability of memorable photographs of the conflict. Over 200 images are employed, adding greatly to the impact of the text.

In happy contrast with many previous publications on the subject, the huge Soviet contribution to the defeat of Germany is given due weight in this book. There is full coverage of the colossal battles of the Eastern Front, which did more than anything else to destroy the fighting power of the German army. Finally, that uniquely appalling aspect of World War II, the Holocaust, is dealt with as an integrated part of the whole. This is just as it should be, as the Holocaust is inextricably bound up with the war itself. It was a war within a war, and, horrifically, was regarded as a completely valid form of military 'duty' by many of its perpetrators. The Holocaust could not have been carried out outside the context of World War II, and its memory remains the grimmest legacy of that terrible conflict.

Paul Cornish

THE CAUSES OF WAR

Historians are still unable to agree as to why World War II came about. The conflict was not simply a question of personal ambition, nor was it a desire for power. There were deeper reasons which can be traced back at least to the settlement forced upon Germany under the terms of the Treaty of Versailles in 1919. As for the Japanese, they had reached a point in their economic and social development which required them to extend their sphere of influence and access to resources beyond the islands which had constrained them for many centuries. In many respects their choice of timing was based on opportunity.

The punitive damages meted out on Germany as the belligerent power during World War I had set a chain of events in motion which caused enormous domestic unrest in Germany. It was also the case that by the 1930s the two most powerful members of the League of Nations were unwilling to back decisions with shows of force: neither Britain nor France was the power it had been just 30 years before. Prior to Adolf Hitler's rise to power Germany had signed the Locarno Treaties in December 1925. They had undertaken to accept the borders which had been laid down in the Treaty of Versailles and agreed that they would never attack France or Belgium again. Germany also accepted that the Rhineland should remain a demilitarized zone. The associated treaties bound France to protect the territorial integrity of Belgium, Czechoslovakia and Poland; as it would transpire, due to Britain's treaties with France, this meant that Britain, too, was guaranteeing their integrity. A further major treaty was signed in 1928 called the Kellogg-Briand Pact, which

▶ *RIGHT: The statue commemorating the establishment of the League of Nations.*

seemed to herald a new era of peace as the 65 signatory countries agreed never to use war again to resolve disputes.

From 1931 the Japanese were involved in attempts to conquer Manchuria. Manchuria's 200,000 sq km (77,000 sq miles) would provide the teeming Japanese population with an area of natural growth and settlement. The League of Nations, despite pleas from the Chinese, did nothing to censure the Japanese.

Between 1935 and 1936, in a desire to create a new African empire for Rome, Benito Mussolini had invaded the technologically backward Abyssinia and had even made the first use of mustard gas. Mussolini had united Abyssinia, Eritrea and Somaliland and now called the area Italian East Africa. Although the League of Nations condemned the Italians, few practical steps were taken to prevent the incursion.

◀ LEFT: Hitler's Nazi army.

Also in 1935, the Germans brought up the thorny issue of rearmament. Hitler wished to reunite and rearm all Germans, but under the term of the Treaty of Versailles he was banned from doing so. Nonetheless, he trebled the size of the army and ordered the construction of aircraft. Little by little Hitler pushed the boundaries of the Treaty of Versailles and the patience of the League of Nations, yet Britain and France in particular stood aside and did not intervene.

The Rhineland crisis of March 1936 could potentially have brought down the wrath of Britain and France on Germany before Hitler was in a position to defend himself. Against strict international agreements, Hitler entered the demilitarized zone with some 32,000 men.

In 1938 the boundaries were pushed once again when the question of Austria arose. Hitler had always considered Austria to be part of Germany anyway, but he knew that simply marching into the country and seizing power would almost certainly result in war. Instead he ensured that Arthur Seyss-Inquart, a prominent Austrian Nazi, was given a senior government position. He then told the Austrian government that they should offer their citizens the opportunity of deciding whether to become one with Germany. Hitler went on to say that if the referendum was not agreed, the Austrian Chancellor Kurt von Schuschnigg should resign. If Schuschnigg did not choose one of these options then Hitler threatened an invasion of Austria. Schuschnigg chose to resign, and his cabinet walked out in support. Only Seyss-Inquart remained and, as the only representative of the government left, he invited Hitler to cross the border.

There was then the question of Czechoslovakia, which had been created in the aftermath of World War I and significantly contained 3.2 million Germans. The Germans lived in the Sudetenland region of the country and earnestly desired to become part of Germany. The Czech government would not agree and Hitler proposed an invasion. Although France had guaranteed Czechoslovakia's territorial integrity, it seemed unlikely that the country would actually move against Germany.

Britain, however, wished to avoid war – they had seen with their own eyes the Spanish Civil War raging from 1936 with most of the future World War II belligerents involved more in fact than in spirit. In British Prime Minister Neville Chamberlain Hitler found a man who was wedded to peace and used this to his advantage. With careful manoeuvring and manipulation Chamberlain was convinced to sign over all parts of Czechoslovakia that had a significant German-speaking population. In the end a deal was concluded between Germany, Britain, France and Italy without once negotiating with the Czechs and on 1 October 1938 Germany occupied Sudetenland.

Hitler, however, was not content with this small area; he also desired Moravia and Bohemia. His claims were based on the fact that the Czechs were ill-treating the half a million German speakers in these regions and that unless the Czech government took immediate action Hitler would take steps to ensure the safety of his people. The Czech government was told that if the German army was not invited across the border to restore law and order then Hitler would have no choice but to bomb Prague. The Czech government caved in and on 15 March 1939 German troops marched into Prague; on the following day Bohemia and Moravia were made protectorates of Germany. All that remained was for Hitler to address the apparent plight of the Germans who now lived within the Polish borders.

Hitler began by cementing his relationships with vital European allies. Italy signed the Pact of Steel with Germany and in August 1939 the final piece in the jigsaw fell into place when the German Foreign Minister Joachim von Ribbentrop and the Russian Premier Vyachelsav

▲ ABOVE: Axis leaders Benito Mussolini and Adolf Hitler.

Molotov signed the German-Russian Pact, which decreed that the two countries would not wage war against each other for a decade. Unknown to all at the time, a clause was included in the Pact which agreed that should either Germany or Russia attack Poland, then the country would be split between them. When Germany finally made that attack on 1 September 1939 there was no more room for manoeuvre. The countries of Europe were past the point of compromise and with great reluctance, two days after Poland was invaded, Britain and France declared war on Germany.

1939

GERMANY INVADES POLAND (1 SEPTEMBER 1939)

Without a formal declaration of war, at 04:45, 53 German divisions began crossing the Polish border. Within a few hours Polish defences had been breached and as German aircraft pounded Polish cities, including Warsaw and Krakow, German tanks penetrated deep into Polish territory. Unbeknown to the Poles or the West, the German-Russian Pact of 23 August had already established a partition line, splitting Poland in two. Germany would also receive Lithuania, whilst Russia would take

Estonia, Latvia, Finland and part of Romania. As soon as the invasion became known, France and British made demands for Germany's immediate withdrawal. By 2 September, after 36 hours, German units had penetrated up to 80 km (50 miles), and had established complete air superiority. Polish resistance was shambolic and instantly broken up by German air attacks.

🔲 *see* Britain and France Declare War p. 19

◀ *LEFT: German troops enter Polish territory.*

ITALY DECLARES ITS NEUTRALITY (2 SEPTEMBER 1939)

The day after Germany's invasion, Italy declared itself to be neutral and called for an international conference to discuss how to halt the war in Poland. On the same day the Germans announced they would not attack Norway provided Germany was not attacked by other countries; the Commonwealth responded by declaring war on Germany. On 4 September Japan declared its neutrality, and the USA followed suit the next day.

◆ *see* US Passes Selective Service Act p. 68

BRITAIN AND FRANCE DECLARE WAR (3 SEPTEMBER 1939)

At 09:00 on 3 September 1939 Sir Neville Henderson, the British Ambassador to Berlin, delivered an ultimatum to Germany stating that unless the country made undertakings to withdraw from Poland by 11:00 that day Britain would consider itself at war. At 12:00 the French Ambassador delivered a similar ultimatum, set to expire the following day. Hitler had been convinced that the western powers would remain neutral after the invasion; now he had to face the prospect of war with Germany's old adversaries.

◆ *see* Prime Minister's Speech to the Nation p. 19

PRIME MINISTER'S SPEECH TO THE NATION (3 SEPTEMBER 1939)

At noon on 3 September 1939 Neville Chamberlain broadcast his speech, informing the nation that Britain's ultimatum to Germany had expired. Germany had not ceased their attack on Poland and as a result, he said 'This country is now at war with Germany. We are ready.' That evening King George VI broadcast to the Commonwealth, stating 'We can only do the right as we see the right, and reverently commit our cause to God'.

◆ *see* Neville Chamberlain p. 20

CHAMBERLAIN, NEVILLE (1869–1940)

Chamberlain had been involved in politics since the early 1900s. In the aftermath of World War I he held a number of senior political posts including Minister of Health (1924–29) and Chancellor of the Exchequer (1931–37). When Chamberlain came to power as Prime Minister (1937), he agreed that the Germans had legitimate grievances arising out of the settlement after World War I. His policies, which became known as 'appeasement', allowed the Anschluss, the union of Germany and Austria in 1938, which had been forbidden by the Treaty of Versailles. When Hitler

demanded control of German-speaking Czechoslovakia (Sudetenland), Chamberlain signed the Munich Agreement, on 29 September 1938. With this, it seemed that war had been avoided, but in March 1939 Hitler seized the rest of Czechoslovakia and Chamberlain realized that Hitler could not be trusted. When German troops rolled across the Polish border in September 1939, Chamberlain was forced to declare war. He proved to be an inept war leader in the ensuing months and he was eventually replaced by Winston Churchill.

◆ see Winston Churchill p. 36

◀ *LEFT: Neville Chamberlain.*

GERMANS CROSS THE VISTULA RIVER (5 SEPTEMBER 1939)

Despite stiffening resistance, the Poles were still unable to stop the
Germans from crossing the Vistula River on 5 September and pressing
their advance on Warsaw. The following day the Germans captured
Krakow and reached the Romanian border. Polish troops were in retreat.
Between 12–18 September 170 Polish prisoners were taken and Warsaw
was surrounded by 15 September. The following day the Germans
demanded surrender, but the Poles refused.

➤ *see* Blitzkrieg p. 21

BLITZKRIEG (1920s-90s)

Blitzkrieg, or 'lightning war', was a concept developed by the British in
the 1920s and supported by the French and German generals Charles
de Gaulle and Heinz Guderian, amongst others, in the 1930s. It had been
originally thought that tanks were only of use in seizing ground by brute
force, but if they could be allowed to smash through enemy lines and
break into the enemy rear, then they could be the ultimate weapon to
avoid the bloody stalemates of the previous war. The Germans used the
Spanish Civil War as a test ground for their new tactics, a devastating
combination of land and air units. When they invaded Poland the
German air force, the Luftwaffe, broke up the Polish defences, whilst the
Panzer tanks broke through and destroyed the enemy's supplies, artillery
and supporting units. Blitzkrieg was used in France, the Balkans, Russia
and North Africa. The tactic was the major contributor to German
successes until 1942. Patton would use his own version of Blitzkrieg, or
mobile warfare, in 1944 against the Germans. The tactic was still being
used in the 1960s and 1970s by the Israelis and by Allied forces during
Operation Desert Storm in 1991.

➤ *see* Soviet Union Invades Poland p. 23

SINKING OF THE HMS *COURAGEOUS* (17 SEPTEMBER 1939)

HMS *Courageous* had been built in 1915 and converted to an aircraft carrier between 1924 and 1928. On 17 September, the German submarine U29 torpedoed her some 240 km (150 miles) off Mizen Head, Ireland. The ship went down in 20 minutes, claiming 518 of her

1,200-man crew, including her captain, W. T. Makeig-Jones. The sinking of the ship was the first loss to the Royal Navy, just two weeks into the war.

see Kriegsmarine p. 22

◀ *LEFT: The HMS* Courageous *was the first naval casualty of the war.*

KRIEGSMARINE (1939–45)

At the outbreak of the war, the German navy was in no position to challenge the Allied fleets. Its major reconstruction plans had just been instituted, the Z-plan had called for 13 battleships or battle cruisers, 4 aircraft carriers, 15 pocket battleships, 23 cruisers and 22 large destroyers. When Germany attacked Poland and the war began, most Z-plan construction was terminated and all available resources were transferred to the building of U-boats. Despite its comparatively small size, the Kriegsmarine managed to achieve some remarkable results, notably in the destruction of several British warships. The tide inevitably turned after the loss of the Bismarck in 1941, surface units were never again used for many offensive operations and every loss served to weaken the German navy. Kriegsmarine U-boat successes continued until 1943, by which time Allied technology and tactics were more than a match for them. By the end of the war only two Kriegsmarine major surface vessels were still operational, the rest had been sunk, irreparably damaged or captured.

◆ *see* Wolf Packs p. 26

SOVIET UNION INVADES POLAND (17 SEPTEMBER 1939)

Under the terms of the German-Russian Pact of 23 August, Russian troops crossed the Polish border, which was largely undefended. German troops evacuated Lvov and Brest-Litovsk in accordance with the agreement with the Soviets. The Polish government fled to Romania, but the Romanians interned them on 18 September. All Polish territory to the east of the River Bug would be ceded to the Soviets, as per their agreement.

◆ *see* Warsaw Surrenders p. 23

WARSAW SURRENDERS (19–28 SEPTEMBER 1939)

Facing little opposition, Russian troops met the German army at Brest-Litovsk. Hitler made a triumphant entry into Danzig on 19 September. After days of bombardment from the air, Warsaw eventually surrendered on 27 September and 160,000 Polish troops were captured. The last of the Polish army, having been encircled since 10 September around Modlin and Kutno, finally surrendered on 28 September. Germany now controlled 22 million Poles and the Russians 13 million.

◆ *see* Soviet Union Invades Poland p. 23

PHONEY WAR (SEPTEMBER 1939)

After Britain and France declared war, many expected that the Germans would make a heavy aerial bombing. Britain constructed shelters, distributed gas masks, put ration plans in action and formed voluntary services (Auxiliary Fire Service and Air Raid Precautions). The Women's Voluntary Service (WVS) started stockpiling clothes and blankets for expected refugees. By mid-September 1.5 million people had evacuated major cities. Despite the preparations, no attack occurred and this period became known as the 'Phoney War'.

▲ ABOVE: The government ordered gas masks for all civilians, expecting immediate raids.

▲ ABOVE: French troops on the Maginot Line.

MAGINOT LINE (1929–40)

The Maginot Line, named after the French Minister of War, was built between 1929 and 1940 and was intended to protect France for long enough to enable the country to mobilize its armies in the event of war. The Maginot Line stretched north from Switzerland to the Ardennes and from the Alps to the Mediterranean. Within vast defence works and hundreds of kilometres of trenches, thousands of men were strung out along the French border. Ultimately the line was extended along the Belgian border, although it was not as strong here. When the Germans struck, they flooded through the 'impenetrable' Ardennes. When the French surrendered, only one Maginot fort had fallen, yet the garrisons were ordered out without having fired a shot. The Maginot Line had been a failure.

WOLF PACKS (1939–43)

The U-boat had almost won World War I for the Germans, yet the country
had just 57 of these submarines, of which only 22 were operationally
effective for service in the Atlantic when war broke out in 1939. Admiral
Karl Doenitz envisaged 'wolf packs' of between 15 to 20 U-boats,
surrounding and sinking Allied merchant convoys. The number of
U-boats gradually increased in the early years of the war and by 1942 there
were more than 100 of them. Initial successes resulted in the sinking of
millions of tons of Allied shipping. Doenitz himself estimated that
700,000 tons of Allied shipping needed to be sunk per month in order
to starve Britain into submission but the wolf packs were struggling to
achieve this target and as 1943 dawned, Allied anti-submarine warfare
and new convoy systems ended the menace of the German wolf pack.
◑ see Sinking of the HMS *Royal Oak* p. 27

GERMANY BEGINS ITS EUTHANASIA PROJECT (OCTOBER 1939)

Since the Nazis had gained power in Germany in 1933, a number of
measures had been taken to ensure 'racial purity'. These included the
forced sterilization of those with mental or physical handicaps and the
murder of infants. In October 1939 Hitler signed an order authorizing
involuntary adult euthanasia. It was signed on his personal stationery to
provide doctors with written protection. The programme, overseen by
Philipp Bouhler and Karl Brandt, directed them to authorize the
euthanasia of primarily non-Jewish Germans. It read: 'Bouhler and Brandt
are instructed to broaden the powers of physicians designated by name,
who will decide whether those who have – as far as can be humanly
determined – incurable illnesses can, after the most careful evaluation,
be granted a mercy death.'
◑ see 10,000 Jews Deported from Vienna p. 86

SINKING OF THE HMS *ROYAL OAK* (14 OCTOBER 1939)

At 27,000 tons, and a cost of £2.5 million, HMS *Royal Oak* was considered virtually unsinkable. Yet on 14 October, the German submarine U47 slipped through the defences at Scapa Flow (Orkney) and sent the *Royal Oak* to the bottom with a salvo of three torpedoes. The great battleship went down in 10 minutes, taking 800 of her crew. It was an immense blow to the Royal Navy and to Britain.

see Battle of the River Plate p. 29

MUNICH PLOT (8 NOVEMBER 1939)

In a plot hatched by Hitler and his Propaganda Minister Paul Joseph Goebbels, a bomb exploded in the Bürgerbräukeller, the famous Munich beer cellar closely associated with the Nazi party. Goebbels blamed British intelligence and the exiled former Nazi, Otto Strasser. This accusation allowed Hitler to eradicate any remaining opposition in Germany. The remnants of the left, church opposition and those in the military were eliminated or brought into line.

see Adolf Hitler p. 54

WINTER WAR (30 NOVEMBER 1939)

Despite the continued Russian territorial claims on Finland, the Russian divisions that began crossing the border on 30 September 1939 came as a great surprise. The Finns, commanded by Carl Gustaf von Mannerheim, may have been hopelessly outnumbered, but they were far superior

▶ *RIGHT: A Russian soldier during the Winter War.*

soldiers to the Russians. By the end of November some 27,500 Russians had been killed. Their leader Joseph Stalin was furious at the lack of progress and ordered in an additional 45 divisions. In temperatures of -30°, the Finns continued to resist, but by February 1940, with 25,000 killed and 43,000 wounded, the Finns were exhausted. The Russo-Finnish Treaty (12 March) saw Finland concede 41,400 sq km (16,000 sq miles) to Russia.

◆ *see* Soviet Union Invades the Baltic States and Romania p. 46

ADMIRAL GRAF SPREE (1936–39)

This German vessel was conceived in 1928, but had a small 10,000 ton limit imposed by the Treaty of Versailles. The ship was officially commissioned in 1936 and dubbed a 'pocket battleship' due to her small

weight and fighting punch. The ship had advanced prototype diesel engines, an electrically welded hull and massive 11-inch guns. As experience would reveal, the weaknesses of such vessels were the thin armour and the decks, a price the German seamen would pay with their lives. The ships were faster than conventional battleships and had the same hitting power as a cruiser.

see Allied Forces Enter Norway p. 33

BATTLE OF THE RIVER PLATE (13–17 DECEMBER 1939)

The *Admiral Graf Spree* slipped into the South Atlantic to claim more Allied shipping, but was spotted by HMS *Ajax*, HMS *Exeter* and HMS *Achilles*. The German ship crippled the *Exeter*, but the other two vessels harried her. Langsdorff, the *Graf Spree*'s captain, turned and headed for the neutral port of Montevideo. With the arrival of HMS *Cumberland*, Langsdorff scuttled his own ship in the estuary, bringing to an end the brief Battle of the River Plate.

see Admiral Graf Spree p. 28

RATIONING BEGINS IN BRITAIN (28 DECEMBER 1939)

By December 1939 German U-boat and surface vessel attacks on Allied shipping had accounted for 746,000 tons, with Britain increasingly isolated from its traditional trading partners. Meat rationing was introduced on 28 December 1939, followed by the rationing of bacon, butter and sugar on 8 January 1940. Each household had to register with their local shops and all animal slaughter ceased whilst the government prepared a livestock-control scheme.

see Blitz Begins p. 66

◄ LEFT: The German battleship Admiral Graf Spree, *sunk during the Battle of the River Plate.*

1940

9 Apr	Germany invades Norway
10 Apr	Allied forces are sent to Norway
10 May	Chamberlain resigns as Prime Minister and Churchill takes over; Germany invades Belgium and Holland
14 May	Germany launches an aerial attack on Rotterdam
15 May	Holland surrenders
27 May	The evacuation of Dunkirk begins
28 May	Belgium surrenders
5 June	The Battle of France begins
9 June	An armistice comes into force in Norway
10 June	Italy declares war
14 June	The Germans enter Paris; Italy invades France
16 June	French Premier Reynaud resigns
17 June	The Soviet Union invades the Baltic States
28 June	De Gaulle becomes leader of the Free French
4 Aug	War begins in East Africa
8 Aug	The Battle of Britain begins
25 Aug	Britain bombs Berlin
7 Sept	The Blitz begins
12 Sept	Italy invades Egypt
16 Sept	The US introduces the Selective Service Act
27 Sept	Germany, Italy and Japan sign the Tripartite Pact
7 Oct	German troops invade Romania
11 Nov	Battle of Taranto
20 Nov	Hungary enters the war
9 Dec	Britain launches its North African offensive

GERMANY STEPS UP WAR PRODUCTION (JANUARY 1940)

In direct contravention to the Treaty of Versailles, Germany had already been systematically increasing its production of military equipment. Not only did the country feel it needed to increase the overall strength of its armed forces, but it also needed to establish the necessary mechanisms to accelerate that production in the future. Between 1938 and 1940, for example, bomber production steadily increased by around 100 bombers per year.

🔹 *see* Germany Invades Demark and Norway p. 32

BRITAIN ISSUES CIVILIAN GAS MASKS (8 MARCH 1940)

Although World War II saw no tactical or strategic use of gas, the British government considered German use of the weapon a distinct possibility. Consequently, from 8 March 1940 all civilians and military personnel were systematically issued with gas masks, including equipment for babies and the infirm. It became a legal obligation to carry a gas mask at all times and gas drills became integral parts of air-raid precaution training.

🔹 *see* Blitz Begins p. 66

GERMANY INVADES DENMARK AND NORWAY (9 APRIL 1940)

On 2 April 1940 Hitler approved Operation Weserübung, the invasion of Norway and Denmark. By 9 April, nine German divisions, covered by the whole German navy and nearly 500 Luftwaffe aircraft, invaded Denmark; it took them only 48 hours to establish control of the country. They also landed at various points in Norway. Britain and France asked the Belgian government to allow their troops to enter Belgium to try and force the Germans back, but the Belgians refused.

🔹 *see* Allied Forces Enter Norway p. 33

ALLIED FORCES ENTER NORWAY (10 APRIL 1940)

On 10 April 1940 a British flotilla attacked 10 German destroyers at the Norwegian port of Narvik. On 13 April, seven German destroyers were sunk in what became known as the Second Battle of Narvik. The first Allied land units began arriving en masse at Narvik two days later. Additional French units landed later in the month, but by the end of April the Germans, advancing from Oslo and Trondheim, retained virtual control of southern Norway.

▲ *ABOVE: French troops embarking for Norway.*

🔹 *see* Norway Surrenders p. 43

KING HAAKON FLEES NORWAY (29 APRIL 1940)

With the Germans in possession of the majority of the southern half of Norway and all the major population centres, King Haakon and his government were evacuated from Andalsnes aboard HMS *Glasgow* on 29 April. They were initially transported to Tromsos in the Arctic Circle, where they established a provisional capital the following day. By 5 May Haakon and his government were in London as the Norwegian situation continued to deteriorate.

QUISLING, VIDKUN (1887–1945)

Quisling was leader of the Norwegian Nasjonal Samling Party, a pro-German fascist group. Despite strong electoral support in the early 1930s, the party's popularity had dwindled by 1940. When Germany invaded Norway, Quisling fully supported the action. In 1942 the German Reichskommisor of Norway, Josef Terboven, named Quisling Minister President (Prime Minister), a post he assumed on 1 February 1943. Although his relationship with Terboven was difficult, Quisling avidly followed German instructions and policies throughout the war. After the surrender of Germany, Quisling and 90,000 members of his party faced charges of treason. Quisling was found guilty of the charges and was executed by firing squad on 24 October 1945.

▲ *ABOVE: Norwegian Fascist Vidkun Quisling, who supported the German invasion.*

CHAMBERLAIN RESIGNS (10 MAY 1940)

In the British House of Commons a debate on the Prime Minister's handling of the Norwegian situation led to a vote which was just narrowly won by Chamberlain. There was, however, sufficient opposition to make his position untenable. Labour and Liberal MPs refused to support the government unless Chamberlain resigned. After three days of political manoeuvring, Chamberlain emerged discredited and unable to gather support; he resigned on 10 May.

◆ *see* Churchill Becomes Prime Minister p. 36

GERMANY INVADES BELGIUM AND HOLLAND (10 MAY 1940)

On 10 May 1940 German airborne units began landing around Rotterdam in Holland and on the pivotal Belgian defence point on the River Meuse, near Liège, Fort Eben Emael. In accordance with the Dyle Plan, the French 7th Army and the British Expeditionary Force entered Belgium to take up positions along the River Dyle. The Germans launched heavy bombing raids against Holland and several of the Belgian towns. With German troops crossing the Meuse either side of Sedan, and the Dutch army close to collapse, what had appeared to be an impregnable Allied line looked increasingly vulnerable.

⬦ *see* Eben Emael p. 38

▲ ABOVE: *German troops in action after crossing the Meuse in May 1940.*

CHURCHILL BECOMES PRIME MINISTER (10 MAY 1940)

With Cromwell's words uttered by Leo Amery 'Depart, I say, and let us have done with you. In the name of God, go' ringing in his ears, Chamberlain resigned on 10 May 1940. Winston Churchill became the only viable candidate, having refused to serve under Chamberlain's preferred successor, Lord Halifax, the Foreign Secretary. Churchill retained Chamberlain in the War Cabinet, the Labour leader Clement Attlee became his Deputy Prime Minister and Halifax remained as Foreign Secretary. Churchill brought in the trade union leader, Ernest Bevin, as Minister of Labour, and the powerful Lord Beaverbrook as Minister for Aircraft Production. Churchill told Parliament 'I have nothing to offer but blood, toil, tears and sweat'.

◆ see Winston Churchill p. 36

CHURCHILL, WINSTON (1874–1965)

Following a successful – if controversial – British army career, Churchill became a war correspondent in 1899. He was elected as an MP the following year and subsequently served in numerous positions between 1906 and 1915; he chose to rejoin the army and served on the Western Front during World War I. Churchill returned to politics after the war, but by 1933 his extreme views on rearmament and his opposition to Hitler's Germany caused his fall from favour in the government. Despite uncertainty about his methods and beliefs, however, Prime Minister Neville Chamberlain appointed Churchill First Lord of the Admiralty in April 1940; a month later Chamberlain resigned and Churchill was asked to form a government.

Churchill developed a strong relationship with the Unites States – a relationship that led to the Lend-Lease Agreement (March 1941). His leadership kept Britain afloat in the early war years and he became something of a hero-figure to the British. After the attack on Pearl Harbor in December 1941, Churchill worked closely with US President Franklin D. Roosevelt to ensure victory over the Axis Powers, welcoming Russia on board to develop a united strategy.

Churchill resisted the opening of a European front in 1943 despite Russian pressure and the collapse of Germany and Italy in North Africa. With victory at hand two years later, Churchill lost power in a landslide Labour victory, but returned in 1951. He retired from public life in 1955 due to ill-health and died on 24 January 1965.

see Italy Declares War on Britain and France p. 44

► RIGHT: Winston Churchill took over the reigns as Prime Minister after Chamberlain's resignation in May 1940.

EBEN EMAEL (11 MAY 1940)

The Belgian fortress of Eben Emael, with its garrison of 1,200 men, was strategically placed on the River Meuse at its junction with the Albert Canal. The fort had been designed to meet every attack – except the method used by the Germans. On 11 May 1940, 80 parachutists landed on the roof of the fort and blew up the gun casements. Having dealt with the defences, the tiny German parachute unit held the garrison in check until German ground forces arrived. More German gliders landed to secure the two key bridges near the fort and by the next day two German Panzer divisions crossed the bridges, precipitating a general Belgian retreat. By 13 May the Germans were poised to swing around the Maginot Line.

see Belgium Surrenders p. 41

DUTCH MONARCH FLEES TO BRITAIN (13 MAY 1940)

With the situation in Holland deteriorating quickly, Dutch troops began moving back to 'Fortress Holland', an area that encompassed Amsterdam, The Hague and Rotterdam. On the same day, Queen Wilhelmina and her government fled Holland for London. On the following day Dutch forces were ordered to stop fighting as the Germans occupied The Hague in an attempt to seize the royal family.

GERMANS BOMB ROTTERDAM (14 MAY 1940)

With an overwhelming air superiority, the Germans subjected Rotterdam to a savage bombardment which claimed at least 800 lives. The attacks, which began at around 13:30 on 14 May, succeeded in breaking the resolve of the Dutch. While Allied aircraft attacked German ground forces, anti-aircraft guns claimed some 85 British and French aircraft in the Sedan area. German general Guderian's tanks, by this stage, were almost all across the River Meuse.

see Holland Surrenders p. 39

HOLLAND SURRENDERS (15 MAY 1940)

Following the intense bombing of Rotterdam the previous day, at 11:00 on 15 May the Dutch army surrendered to Germany. The front in Belgium appeared to be stabilizing, but by the next day Erwin Rommel's 7th Armoured Division had penetrated 85 km (50 miles) into French territory and was heading for Cambrai, having captured 10,000 prisoners and 100 tanks. Between 17 and 19 May, de Gaulle's 4th Armoured Division attempted to stop Guderian just north of Laon. The counterattack failed and Brussels was declared an open city. Shortly afterwards the Germans took Antwerp.

◆ see Belgium Surrenders p. 41

OSWALD MOSLEY IS INTERNED (19 MAY 1940)

Sir Oswald Mosley, leader of the British Union of Fascists, was arrested and imprisoned along with 33 other prominent Fascists. Following this move, there was a series of other arrests and restrictions placed on the movement of 3,000 German-born citizens and 11,000 other aliens. All male aliens were required to report to the police each day and to stay inside their homes between 20:00 and 06:00 hours.

◆ see Pétain and Vichy France p. 47

◀ LEFT: A German air force farewell salute before taking off to attack the enemy.

GERMANS REACH THE ENGLISH CHANNEL (20 MAY 1940)

At around 09:00 on 20 May 1940 Guderian took Amiens and 11 hours later his advanced units reached the English Channel at Noyelles in France. Trapped to the north was the French 1st Army, nine divisions of the British Expeditionary Force and the entire Belgian army. Some 45 Allied divisions had been surrounded by this time. The following day, British armour attempted to break through the German lines at Arras. Two French divisions attacked towards Cambrai, but both offensives failed. German forces turned north towards Boulogne and Calais; more Allied counterattacks failed and the Germans continued to advance between 23 and 25 May. There was little coordination between the British, French and Belgian efforts and on 25 May Boulogne fell, trapping the Allied armies.

◆ *see* Dunkirk Evacuates p. 40

DUNKIRK EVACUATES (27 MAY–4 JUNE 1940)

Codenamed Operation Dynamo, under RAF air cover, the Allies began the evacuation of Dunkirk on 27 May. They extricated 338,266 men, of which 120,000 were French or Belgian. Waves of German attacks took place around the

◀ *LEFT: Germans in Dunkirk after the British evacuation in 1940, codenamed Operation Dynamo.*

perimeter as more and more men were evacuated. Some 200 ships were lost during the operation; the British alone left 60,000 trucks and 2,000 guns, as well as thousands of tons of fuel and ammunition. The last ship to leave Dunkirk was the destroyer Shikari and by dawn on 4 June German troops were standing on the Dunkirk beach. The last 4,000 British soldiers had been evacuated two days previously, by which time the French rearguard was little more than two miles from the Dunkirk beach. Bereft of arms and equipment, Churchill realized that the Germans would ultimately attempt to land and take Britain itself. In his immortal speech he said 'We shall fight on the beaches ... we shall fight in the fields ... we shall never surrender'.

◼ *see* Germans Occupy Paris p. 45

BELGIUM SURRENDERS (28 MAY 1940)

The British and the French were informed that the Belgian army was close to collapse. The Belgian government asked King Leopold to leave the country, but he refused. At 17:00 Leopold sent an envoy to the German headquarters, offering surrender. He received a reply at 22:00, telling him that Hitler demanded an unconditional surrender and Leopold signed at 12:30 on 28 May; this is now repudiated by the Belgian government in Paris.

◼ *see* Germany Invades Belgium and Holland p. 35

THE PANZERS (1930S–1945)

The early German tanks were no match for either the French or British armoured fighting vehicles – in firepower at least. They were, however, considerably faster, more manoeuvrable and, above all, deployed in concentrated numbers, rather than the British and French habit of spreading them out amongst infantry units. The German Panzer I was

▲ *ABOVE: The German Panzer.*

little more than a fast-moving machine-gun unit, whereas the Panzer II and Panzer III had limited firepower of no more than 20 mm (0.8 in). The Germans had received a considerable bonus when they occupied Czechoslovakia because they had acquired the vast Skoda factory and its technically superior 38T tank. Large numbers of these Czech vehicles were deployed by the German army in their drive through the Lowlands and France.

◆ *see* Battle of France p. 42

BATTLE OF FRANCE (5–25 JUNE 1940)

On 5 June 1940, preceded by a ferocious bombardment along the River Somme and the Aisne, a series of German thrusts were made on the French lines. By the following day German troops had broken through in the Amiens area and had reached the flank of the Maginot Line. On 7 June the Germans were just short of Rouen on the River Seine and two days later they had occupied the city, as well as Dieppe; they had also reached the River Marne. French troops were in retreat around the Somme and the whole army seemed to be on the verge of collapse. By 10 June the French government fled as German troops advanced on Paris. The following day Paris was declared an open city and on 14 June German troops entered the capital. Verdun was taken on 15 June and on 17 June Guderian's tanks had almost reached the Swiss border.

GUDERIAN, HEINZ (1888–1954)

A Prussian General's son, Guderian was a career soldier who studied tank tactics. He gained experience in the years leading up to World War II by commanding a motorized battalion and, later, the 2nd Panzer Division. He and his troops were the leaders of the invasion of Poland in 1939. He also led the 2nd Panzer Group in the invasion of Russia in 1941, but after disagreements with his superiors, he was dismissed in December of the same year. Guderian was recalled in March 1943, but in July lost disastrously at the Battle of Kirsk. He became commander of the General Staff in July 1944, but argued with Hitler over military strategy, and found himself dismissed again. Captured by US troops in May 1945, the Russians and Poles demanded he face war-crime charges, but Guderian was eventually released in June 1948 and died in 1954.

▲ *ABOVE: Heinz Guder*

◆ *see* Germans Reach the English Channel p. 40

NORWAY SURRENDERS (9 JUNE 1940)

When King Haakon and his government left Tromso aboard the HMS *Devonshire*, heading for the safety of London, the way was clear for a German victory in Norway. On 9 June the last Allied troops left Norway and an armistice came into force there. For the next four years the country would live under German occupation, although it would be ostensibly ruled via Quisling, a Norwegian collaborator with the Germans.

◆ *see* Germans Occupy Paris p. 45

ITALY DECLARES WAR ON BRITAIN AND FRANCE (10 JUNE 1940)

With the situation in France deteriorating and the French government leaving Paris for Tours, information was received that Italy would soon throw itself into the arena of war on the side of the Germans. At 16:30 on 10 June, the Italian Foreign Minister Ciano informed the French Ambassador that Italy considered itself at war with France, a situation that would come into effect the following day. At 16:45 the Italian minister sent a similar message to the British Ambassador.

see Italy Invades France p. 46

ITALIAN BOMBING OFFENSIVE (11–12 JUNE 1940)

On 11 June the Italian air force bombed Port Sudan and Aden, while the RAF carried out retaliatory attacks on Italian troops based in Eritrea. Meanwhile the Italians launched eight air raids on Malta. The following day the RAF hit Turin and Genoa. Disaster struck later in the month, though, when Italian anti-aircraft guns shot down the Italian governor of Libya over Tobruk, whilst he was returning from a reconnaissance flight.

REYNAUD APPEALS FOR US INTERVENTION (13 JUNE 1940)

The French Premier, Paul Reynaud, having turned down calls for an armistice on 12 June, met Winston Churchill for the last time the following day. He sent an urgent appeal to the United States, asking them to 'throw the weight of American power into the scales in order to save France, the advanced guard of democracy'. Reynaud was under increasing pressure from his own council of ministers.

see Pétain and Vichy France p. 47

▶ RIGHT: *German troops ride through the conquered French capital.*

GERMANS OCCUPY PARIS (14 JUNE 1940)

With Paris declared an open city at 07:00 on 14 June, German motorcyclists rode into the capital, closely followed by support units. The Armée de Paris had scattered and the French government had fled the capital four days previously. In all, some two million Parisians evacuated the city, harassed on their way by German aircraft. Within a few hours the Swastika was flying from the Eiffel Tower and the Arc de Triomphe and German troops were marching down the Champs Elysée for the first time since 1871. Across the city, cinemas, restaurants and other buildings had signs attached to them, reserving them for German troops. Any Frenchman who refused to cooperate met immediate, uncompromising force from the Germans.

◆ see France Signs an Armistice with Italy and Germany p. 47

ITALY INVADES FRANCE (14 JUNE 1940)

With the Maginot Line breached and the French in retreat, the Italians crossed the Alps and attacked the French on 14 June. By 20 June German units had moved to assist the Italians and on the same day France requested an armistice with Italy. On 22 June the Italians occupied Menton.

see France Signs an Armistice with Italy and Germany p. 47

SOVIET UNION INVADES THE BALTIC STATES AND ROMANIA (17 JUNE 1940)

The Russian army marched into Lithuania unopposed on 17 June 1940 in accordance with the agreements they had made with the Germans. Some 35,000 Germans living in Lithuania began moving west. On 21 July Lithuania, Latvia and Estonia agreed to become part of Russia. On 28 June Russian troops crossed the Romanian border to claim Bukovina and Bessarabia. The Romanian King Carol abdicated on 6 September.

see Germans Enter Romania p. 71

FRANCE SIGNS AN ARMISTICE WITH ITALY AND GERMANY (22 JUNE 1940)

As a final act of humiliation for the French, the Germans insisted that they sign the armistice in the same railway coach in which the Germans received the armistice demands from General Foch in November 1918. Hitler sat on the same chair used by Foch when he presented General Charles Huntziger the document. If anything, it was more punitive than the one Germany had signed in 1918.

◻ see Pétain and Vichy France p. 47

PÉTAIN AND VICHY FRANCE (1940–44)

Vichy France (État français) was the term used to describe the French government led by Henri Philippe Pétain and based in Vichy (south-east of Paris), which co-operated with Germany between 1940 and 1944. Pétain came to power on 16 June and signed the surrender document on 22 June. France would have an occupied and unoccupied zone; all Jews were to be handed over to the Germans; French prisoners of war would not be released; and the French would bear the cost of the German occupation.

The Vichy regime was formally established on 10 July. Pétain remained in power until 20 August 1944. Joseph Darnand, head of the Vichy Milice (police) held an SS rank and pledged allegiance to Germany. He suppressed the Resistance Movement and supported German race laws. The Vichy regime deported over 70,000 Jews and sent 650,000 workers to Germany.

◻ see De Gaulle Becomes Free French Leader p. 49

◀ *LEFT: The historic railway carriage where the French signed the armistice in June 1940, surrounded by a German guard of honour.*

DE GAULLE BECOMES FREE FRENCH LEADER (28 JUNE 1940)

With French troops still fighting the Germans in France, Charles de Gaulle made a radio broadcast in London in which he declared that the war was not over and that the battle for France was a part of the war. He invited all French in England to join him in continuing the struggle but received little support or enthusiasm. The following day he made another broadcast from London, making it clear that he did not support the government of Pétain and would not abide by his decisions. On 23 June he made a further broadcast proposing the creation of the French National Committee. Five days later he was recognized as 'the leader of all free Frenchmen'.

◖ *see* Charles de Gaulle p. 49

DE GAULLE, CHARLES (1890–1970)

De Gaulle was wounded twice during World War I. In the 1930s he fell out of favour in France, but was a major tank commander by May 1940. In June he was appointed Minister of War, but when Pétain assumed power de Gaulle was sentenced to death and fled to England. Until 1943 he sought to unite the French resistance and formed the French Committee of National Liberation. De Gaulle was left out of Allied decision-making, but Britain and the US recognized his claims in July 1944. The following month de Gaulle's 2nd Armoured Division entered Paris. On 13 November 1945 de Gaulle was officially recognized as head of the French government. Between 1946 and 1969, though, de Gaulle's power fluctuated; he continued to adopt right-wing policies, seeking to regain French power and independence. He retired in 1969 to complete his memoirs and died on 9 November 1970.

◖ *see* British Sink French Fleet in Oran p. 51

◄ *LEFT: Free French leader Charles de Gaulle.*

GERMANY INVADES THE CHANNEL ISLANDS (30 JUNE 1940)

On 28 June 1940 the Channel Islands were partially evacuated and demilitarized and two days later German troops began landing on Jersey and Guernsey. Britain had taken the decision not to contest the two islands, as large numbers of the islanders, their property and animals had already been evacuated. A considerable number of the population chose to stay, as did many police officers and parts of the civilian administration.

◆ *see* Battle of Britain p. 52

▲ *ABOVE: A captured British flag from Guernsey is sent back to Germany.*

BRITISH SINK THE FRENCH FLEET IN ORAN (3 JULY 1940)

The British launched Operation Catapult on 3 July 1940, aiming to prevent the French fleet from falling into German hands. The French commander was given a six-hour ultimatum to surrender his ships either to Britain or to the US; he failed to respond. Consequently several French ships were sunk or damaged and 1,300 French sailors lost their lives. On the same day over 200 French vessels were seized in British ports. Following the attack, Pétain's Vichy government broke off diplomatic relations with Great Britain.

🔵 *see* Allies Attack Dakar p. 69

DER KANALKAMPF (10 JULY 1940)

On 10 July 1940, the sporadic German attacks on the Channel convoys began to intensify; this would signal the first phase of the Battle of Britain. For 10 days the Luftwaffe dropped mines into the harbours and shipping channels at night and attacked the convoys during the day. Dowding's Fighter Command committed several squadrons to defence, but he refused to significantly weaken the fighter cover for Britain itself.

The latter half of July was marked by bad weather and poor visibility, but by 8 August attacks had grown once more – 18 merchant ships and four Royal Navy destroyers had been lost. By this time, the Luftwaffe had lost some 248 aircraft against 148 RAF losses.

HITLER BROADCASTS A PEACE OFFER TO BRITAIN (19 JULY 1940)

Hitler, addressing the Reichstag in Berlin, made a direct and final appeal to Britain: 'If the struggle continues it can only end in annihilation for one of us. Mr Churchill thinks it will be Germany. I know it will be Britain. I am not the vanquished begging for mercy. I speak as a victor. I can see no reason why this war must go on.'

🔵 *see* Adolf Hitler p. 54

BATTLE OF BRITAIN (AUGUST 1940)

The Battle of Britain began in August 1940 as the first stage in the German preparations for invading Britain. The Luftwaffe attacks had three objectives: Kanalkampf, aimed to interdict merchant convoys; Adlergriff, aimed at destroying RAF and warning infrastructure; and Adlertag, which hoped to destroy ports and airfields. In all, some 12,039 sorties were flown, 11,000 tons of high explosive and 616 tons of incendiary bombs were dropped.

On 16 September, the Germans had estimated RAF fighter strength to be no more than 300 aircraft (in fact there were 579 Spitfires and Hurricanes). Between August and September the RAF estimated German losses at 1,600 aircraft with a possible 500 more. Fighter Command had lost around 900 aircraft. Total civilian losses between July and December 1940 have been estimated at around 23,002 dead and 32,138 wounded.

On 19 September, Operation Seelöwe – the planned German invasion – was postponed indefinitely. The victory prompted Churchill to utter the immortal words 'Never in the field of human conflict has so much been owed by so many to so few'. Nonetheless, the Germans came close to overcoming the RAF and only the sudden switch to terror raids on cities gave the RAF their vital breathing space.

DOWDING, HUGH (1882–1970)

Dowding was originally an army officer, but served as the commander of 16 Squadron of the Royal Flying Corps during World War I, joining the newly formed Royal Air Force in the interwar years, and being promoted to Air Marshal in 1933. He was instrumental in the development of the Spitfire, Hurricane and radar, and ultimately took over control of Fighter Command. Dowding successfully argued that the development of fighter defences was imperative in the impending war against the German

Luftwaffe. Against enormous opposition, Dowding refused to fritter away Britain's air defences over France, but he did cover the Dunkirk evacuation.

Dowding's tactical abilities led to victory in the Battle of Britain, despite being criticized for lack of aggression by many prominent figures. He was replaced by one of his sternest critics, William Sholto Douglas. Dowding was given an official post in the United States until he formally retired in July 1942. Between 1943 and 1951 he wrote five books. Dowding died in February 1970.

see Hitler Broadcasts a Peace Offer to Britain p. 51

▲ *ABOVE: Air Marshal Sir Hugh Dowding.*

OPERATION SEELÖWE (AUGUST 1940)

German plans for an invasion of Britain were formulated in July 1940. The invasion was to be codenamed Operation Seelöwe ('Sea-Lion') and was designed to be launched in mid-September. Landings would be made in the Dover area; two airborne divisions would land first to secure the area, following by nine other divisions, which would cross the English Channel in converted river barges. Preparations were due to be completed by late August.

Success required the Luftwaffe to defeat the RAF and then deal with the Royal Navy – any other outcome would mean that the invasion was doomed. Whether Hitler ever took the invasion seriously is unclear; Churchill certainly did not – he actually sent troops to North Africa during this period. The Luftwaffe failed in their objectives and on 19 September, Operation Seelöwe was indefinitely postponed.

◆ *see* Battle of Britain p. 52

HITLER, ADOLF (1889–1945)

As a soldier during World War I, Hitler won the Iron Cross, but only achieved the rank of Corporal. He was in hospital recovering from a gas attack when Germany surrendered in 1918. By the early 1920s he was involved in right-wing German politics and in 1923 attempted a coup, known as the Munich Beer Hall Putsch. He was imprisoned, but released in 1924. The Nazi Party became the second largest force in German politics by 1930 and it had gained the majority by 1932. Hitler became Chancellor in January 1933. Rounding up opponents, breaking up meetings, crushing the Communists and trade unions, by the end of 1933 150,000 people had been sent to camps. Hitler began regaining German prestige, rejoining with Austria in 1938, seizing Czechoslovakia and then invading Poland in 1939. By the end of 1940, Hitler had humbled the Allies and was ready to turn on Russia. As German troops took territories, Nazi policies of submission and liquidation ravaged Europe. However, Hitler's powers began to decline after the Seige of Stalingrad in 1943; the Führer, as he was known, started suffering from insomnia, tremor and spasms, and blaming others for his failures. He married his mistress, Eva Braun, two days before committing suicide as the Russians arrived in Germany on 30 April 1945.

◆ *see* Britain's First Bombing Raid on Berlin p. 66

▲ ABOVE: German leader Adolf Hitler making a radio broadcast.

WAR IN EAST AFRICA (4 AUGUST 1940–27 NOVEMBER 1941)

The war officially reached East Africa on 4 August 1940. The Italian attack on British Somalia led to the capture of Berbera on 19 August 1940. Throughout September the Italians were harassed by British air raids. It was not until 19 January 1941, however, that British forces in Sudan launched their counteroffensive. Sir William Platt had just two divisions with which to face 17,000 Italians. Two days later the Italians were in retreat, heading for the fortress of Keren. They were intercepted on 3 February but Italian reserves had moved up and successfully pushed the British back on 12 February. On 23 February Free French forces landed in Eritrea and the British crossed the Juba River, capturing Mogadishu the following day. On 16 March British troops arriving from Aden drove the Italians out of Berbera and fresh British troops crossed the Ethiopian border and reached Jijiga. On 27 March the battle for Keren – having lasted almost eight weeks – was over, 3,000 Italians were dead and resistance was crushed. The following day the Italians retreated towards Addis Ababa, which fell to the British on 6 April. By now the British had advanced 1,700 miles. The final Italian garrison would surrender on 27 November.

◆ see Renewed German Offensive and Gazala Line p. 148

ADLERANGRIFF (8 AUGUST 1940)

At the beginning of August Hitler had issued Directive 1, in which he ordered Goering's Luftwaffe to destroy the RAF. Adlerangriff ('Attack of the Eagles') was the codename for the operation.

Luftwaffe squadrons were concentrated around the Calais region in preparation, but the British had already cracked the enigma codes and were desperately decoding the vast flood of orders to the German squadrons. Despite the fact that up to this point German aircraft losses had reached some 2,600, with British losses almost the same, the Germans still underestimated British aircraft-production capacity.

In early morning of 8 August, 300 Stukas and 150 Me109s headed for a British convoy en route to Swanage in Dorset. The plan was to draw out the RAF and destroy them over the Channel. Several Spitfire and Hurricane squadrons engaged the Me109s while the Stukas hit the ships. Another Luftwaffe attack took place at around 16:30 with over 150 German aircraft involved. RAF losses had been 13, Luftwaffe losses 16. This was an unsubstantial rate of attrition; the RAF knew it – and so did Goering's Luftwaffe.

◆ see Stuka p. 59

▲ ABOVE: Stuka planes in the German Luftwaffe on a raid.

GOERING, HERMANN (1893–1946)

An air ace with 22 kills to his name, Goering had been awarded the Iron Cross during World War I. He was recruited into the Nazi Party in 1922, and was involved in the Munich Beer Hall Putsch of 1923. Goering fled Germany after the coup, returning in 1927 and working to bring the Nazis to power. Goering was made Commander-in-Chief of the Luftwaffe in 1935 and directed campaigns against Poland (1939) and France (1940).

The Luftwaffe began their air assault on Britain in August 1940, as a prelude to the planned invasion. They failed, however, and Hitler never forgave Goering. From 1943 the Luftwaffe came under increasing pressure, reduced as it was to defensive operations against the growing

air power of the Allies. Goering sank into depression, undermined by others now closer to Hitler, who decreed he would remain in Berlin until the end. Goering mistook this as a signal to seize the reins of power in Germany, but instead was dismissed from his posts, expelled from the Nazi Party and subsequently arrested. Captured by US troops in May 1945, Goering was a key figure at the Nuremberg trials. He was found guilty on four counts of war crimes and sentenced to death by hanging. On 5 October 1946, two hours before his scheduled execution, he committed suicide in his cell.

◆ see Battle of Britain p. 52

◀ LEFT: Hermann Goering.

STUKA (1937–45)

The Junkers Ju87 'Stuka', known to the Germans as Sturzkampf-bomber, was a dive bomber, effective against ships and tanks. Full-scale production began in 1937; early versions could carry a single 250 kg (550 lb) bomb plus four 50 kg (110 lb) bombs under the wings. The Stuka had proved to be devastating in Poland, France and the Low Countries, but over the English Channel and southern England it was no match for the Spitfire or the Hurricane. Its primary role was to break up enemy concentrations, paving the way for German ground troops. Its terrifying dive to attack was accompanied by screaming sirens fitted to the aircraft for added shock value. Ultimately, the accuracy of the bombs depended on pilot skill, though. Defensively it had two front-mounted machine guns and a rear-mounted gun manned

▶ *RIGHT: German Stuka planes.*

by a second crew member. Whole squadrons of the Stuka were destroyed
by the RAF and they were withdrawn from the area of operations, but
continued in action elsewhere. The Stuka had a maximum speed of just
314 kph (195 mph) and a range of 320 km (199 miles), making it easy prey
for most Allied fighters.

■ *see* Germans Target Radar Stations p. 60

GERMANS TARGET RADAR STATIONS (11 AUGUST 1940)

On 11 August 1940 the first major German air offensive was ready to
begin. The Luftwaffe could muster 2,669 bombers and 933 fighters
(Me109s). Against this was ranged 704 RAF fighters, over 600 of which
were Hurricanes and Spitfires. The RAF also had 350 bombers. On the
same day the Germans began daytime attacks on radar stations in the
south-east and along the south coast of Britain, notably in Portland
and Weymouth.

ME110 (1936–45)

The Me110, or Messerschmitt BF110, was originally designed as a fighter
plane to clear the path of incoming bomber streams. The aircraft was
nicknamed the 'Destroyer'. It was used to some effect against Channel
convoys, but it was no match for Spitfires or Hurricanes. It was reduced
to the role of fighter bomber due to its long range (1,720 km/1,070
miles) with a speed of 467 kph (290 mph). The first Me110 flew in 1936
and was gradually improved; it was still in production in 1945, by which
time some 6,500 had been built. The BF110C saw the most service
during the Battle of Britain, where it suffered heavily at the hands of
RAF pilots. This version of the aircraft had a maximum speed of 402 kph
(250 mph).

■ *see* Stuka p. 59

▲ ABOVE: The German Messerschmitt Me110, nicknamed 'The Destroyer'.

ADLERTAG (13 AUGUST 1940)

Adlertag ('Eagle Day') was the codename given to the phase of the Battle of Britain that saw an intensification of raids against key air-defence targets. The raids, launched on 13 August, were the heaviest the Luftwaffe had been able to muster. In excess of 1,400 German aircraft flew over the English Channel in waves, with orders to destroy all RAF airbases in south-east England, paving the way for Operation Sealion. Once the RAF had been destroyed, the Germans could concentrate on British naval targets.

Despite being hugely outnumbered, the RAF accounted for 45 German aircraft losses with just 13 of its own. All but two of the RAF bases were saved, in the north of the country a further 15 German aircraft were destroyed on diversionary raids for no loss.

Hitler was furious with the failure of the Luftwaffe, yet the pounding continued throughout August and into September when, unbelievably, just as the RAF was on its knees, the Luftwaffe began air attacks aimed at London. While the Luftwaffe pummelled the capital, the RAF recovered and it became evident that the invasion would never happen; after four months of raids, the Luftwaffe had failed.

▲ *ABOVE: The German Messerschmitt Me109.*

ME109 (1935–45)

The Messerschmitt Me109, also known as the BF-109, was the primary German fighter aircraft between 1935 and 1942. For its time it was revolutionary in the sense that it was easy to construct, small and driven by a powerful engine. Early versions had performance problems, but these were resolved in service during the Spanish Civil War. During this early period, it faced out-dated bi-planes, but the new version in 1937 broke the air-speed record, clocking up 610.43 kph (379.07 mph). By 1943, however, particularly on the Western Front, it had been replaced by the Focke-Wulf 190. The Me109 stayed in service in large numbers in the Mediterranean, over Italy and North Africa. It has been estimated that around 35,000 Me109s had been built by 1945. The Me109s finest hour occurred during the sprawling air battles over the English Channel and southern England in 1940, when the German aces locked horns with the RAF Spitfires and Hurricanes.

When handled by an experienced pilot, the Me109 was a highly manoeuvrable aircraft, but it had restricted vision, poor landing (due to thin wheels) and could not be fitted with heavy armaments without affecting its speed and handling.

�«» *see* Me110 p. 60

SPITFIRE (1938–45)

The Spitfire was based on the Supermarine S6B seaplane and came into service with the RAF in 1938. It was continually modified, the first version having a speed of 580 kph (360 mph) and the last, the Spitfire XIV, 710 kph (440 mph). The initial orders, placed before September 1939, amounted to 1,160. The Spitfire became the symbol and the hammer of victory during the Battle of Britain, winning the hearts and minds of pilots and the public. By the end of the war, some 20,000 had been built.

In September 1939 the RAF held sufficient Spitfires to provide nine squadrons with them; just a year previously, the RAF had barely a single squadron. The Spitfire XIV shot down 300 V1 doodle-bugs in 1944 alone. The aircraft was a fighter, yet they were capable of carrying a 110–220 kg (250–500 lb) bomb under the fuselage and a 110 kg (250 lb) bomb under each wing. The aircraft became immortalized as the symbol of British resistance and resolve in the darkest times of the war.

◐ *see* Britain's First Bombing Raid on Berlin p. 66

▲ *ABOVE: The British Spitfire.*

ITALY CONQUERS BRITISH SOMALILAND (19 AUGUST 1940)

The Italians launched their attack on British Somaliland on 4 August, moving in three columns. The tiny British force could only harass the overwhelming numbers of Italian troops, hitting exposed units and striking at lines of communication. By 19 August the Italians had occupied Berbera, the capital, but British resistance continued in the mountains. Ten days later Commonwealth forces began a series of raids to dislodge the Italians.

◐ *see* Italy Invades Egypt p. 67

'NEVER IN THE FIELD OF HUMAN CONFLICT' (21 AUGUST 1940)

On 21 August 1940, as the RAF held off the German Luftwaffe in the skies over the English Channel, Winston Churchill delivered a defiant speech, recognizing that this war was a continuation of the previous one, but that this time it depended on organization, strategy, science and morale. He gave his utmost praise to the RAF, saying 'Never in the field of human

▼ *BELOW: An RAF attack during the Battle of Britain.*

conflict was so much owed by so many to so few. All hearts go out to the fighter pilots, whose brilliant actions we see with our own eyes day after day, but we must never forget that all the time ... our bomber squadrons travel far into Germany, find their targets in the darkness by the highest navigational skill, aim their attacks, with deliberate, careful precision, and inflict shattering blows upon the ... structure of the Nazi power.'

◆ see Winston Churchill p. 36

BRITAIN'S FIRST BOMBING RAID ON BERLIN (25 AUGUST 1940)

In retaliation for attacks on London, the RAF dropped bombs and leaflets over Berlin on the night of 25 August, remaining over the city for three hours. Although the raid was ineffective, it shocked the Germans and Hitler was furious with Goering, who had promised that such a raid could never take place. It was a great boost to British morale.

◆ see Hitler Begins the Blockade of Britain p. 68

BLITZ BEGINS (7 SEPTEMBER 1940)

From July 1940 the Luftwaffe concentrated its efforts on eliminating the RAF by targeting radar stations, aircraft factories, airfields and tackling RAF fighters in the air. This period, known as the Battle of Britain, had been a failure, but the RAF was on the verge of collapse. Suddenly, on 7 September, the Luftwaffe changed its tactics and began to target London, signalling the beginning of the Blitz.

On the first day, 430 civilians were killed and 1,600 wounded; another 412 were killed the following day. Although the Blitz would continue at a lower intensity throughout the war years, it is the period up to May 1941 that signifies the Blitz phase. During this time 130 large-scale night raids were made on Britain, some 71 against London alone. Other targets included key industrial cities across the country.

The Blitz claimed the lives of some 60,000 civilians; a further 87,000 were injured and two million homes were destroyed. London was worst hit with 60 per cent of the casualties and damage. By the time the war had reached its mid-point, the number of British civilian deaths had outweighed loses in military manpower.

 *see* Bombing of Coventry p. 78

ITALY INVADES EGYPT (12 SEPTEMBER 1940)

On the night of 12 September 1940, Italian

▲ *ABOVE: British civilians salvage what they can from the wreckage during the Blitz.*

troops crossed the Egyptian border from Libya and occupied Sollum. Within four days they had reached Sidi Barrani, despite heavy losses as a result of RAF bombing. On 25 September British aircraft raided Tobruk and their naval forces bombarded Sidi Barrani. Italian forces were static and when Hitler met with Italian leader Mussolini at the beginning of the following month, he offered Italy military aid in North Africa; Mussolini declined.

 *see* Rudolfo Graziana p. 68

US PASSES THE SELECTIVE SERVICE ACT (16 SEPTEMBER 1940)

The Selective Service Act, established on 16 September 1940, was the first US peacetime draft in the country's history. Significantly, under US law, this was not 'involuntary servitude' under the terms of the 13th Amendment, but rather the US Congress's right to raise and support an army. Remarkably, and again for the first time in US history, African-American troops would be included in the drafts. 16.1 million US citizens would serve.

▶ see Roosevelt is Re-Elected p. 74

HITLER BEGINS THE BLOCKADE OF BRITAIN (17 SEPTEMBER 1940)

With the Luftwaffe unable to eliminate the RAF, let alone bomb Britain into submission, Hitler realized that the prospect of launching an invasion was slipping through his fingers. By coordinating the U-boat effort, the judicious use of German surface vessels and continued pressure from the Luftwaffe, he intended to starve Britain into submission. At the very least, Hitler hoped that he could render the bellicose Churchill unable to take any action against German interests in Europe or elsewhere. Indeed, without food and materials support from North America and beyond, the island had little hope of being able to feed or defend itself in the long term.

▶ see Blitz Begins p. 66

GRAZIANA, RUDOLFO (1882–1955)

Graziana later became the Marshal of Italy, but between 1926 and 1930 he was the Vice-Governor of Cyrenaica and Libya, afterwards rising to the post of Governor until 1934. During 1935 and 1936 he served as the Governor of Somalia and after that until 1939 he was the Viceroy of Ethiopia. He became the Italian Chief of General Staff in 1939, a post he held until 1941 while simultaneously serving as the Governor General for Libya and the Commander-in-Chief for Italian forces in North Africa. Mussolini effectively sidelined him after his defeat but he returned as the Minister of War for the Socialist Republic of Italy after Mussolini had been deposed. At the same time, he served as the General Commanding Officer of the Ligurian Army.

◆ *see* British Launch an Offensive in North Africa p. 80

ALLIES ATTACK DAKAR (23 SEPTEMBER 1940)

The attack on Vichy-held Dakar was de Gaulle's first major operation. He had hoped that the Vichy would offer no resistance in West Africa. At 07:00 on 23 September he made a radio broadcast, asking for permission to land. He repeated it an hour later and then made a third request. At 10:50 Vichy coastal batteries opened up and attempts to land were checked. The action was called off.

◆ *see* Jacques Leclerc p. 69

LECLERC, JACQUES (1902–47)

French Captain Leclerc was seriously wounded near the River Aube in 1940. He escaped capture, fleeing to Spain and England, and joining de Gaulle's Free French movement. As a major in Cameroon, he took the country from Vichy forces and became Commandant of Chad, launching raids against the Italians in Libya. Leclerc fought as a subordinate,

▶ *RIGHT: French military leader Jacques Leclerc.*

independent commander under General Montgomery in North Africa, and then moved to Patton's command in France (August 1944). Leclerc's men were honoured to be the first Allied troops to enter liberated Paris on 25 August 1944, and were involved in the offensives against Germany itself. After the war in Europe ended, Leclerc was assigned to the Far East, but arrived too late; the Japanese had already surrendered. Leclerc was killed in an aircraft crash in November 1947.

◆ *see* Operation Torch p. 183

▲ ABOVE: *Axis leaders give the fascist salute after signing the Tripartite Pact.*

TRIPARTITE PACT (27 SEPTEMBER 1940)

The Tripartite Pact, signed between Germany, Italy and Japan, on 27 September 1940, was ratified in Berlin. The pact obliged the three countries to come to one another's military assistance in the case of any attack by a country not already involved in the war. The Italians and Germans would have a free hand to establish a new order in Europe, while the Japanese would have similar freedoms in Asia.

◆ *see* Italy Fails in Greece p. 73

GERMANS ENTER ROMANIA (7 OCTOBER 1940)

German troops entered Romania on the pretext of restructuring the Romanian military, but in fact they were hoping to secure the Romanian oil wells. Five days later Mussolini learned of the coup and reportedly said 'Hitler always presents me with a *fait accompli*, but this time I shall pay him back in his own coin. When he reads the papers he'll see that I've occupied Greece, and that will make us all square.'

◆ *see* Italy Fails in Greece p. 73

AMERICANS REGISTER FOR THE DRAFT (16 OCTOBER 1940)

The 1940 Selective Service Act had netted the US with around 16 million men by 16 October of that year. Ultimately around 8.5 million would be assigned to the US army, 3.5 to the US navy and half a million to the marines. These men would assume largely front-line duties. The remainder and large numbers of women would be assigned non-combat or specialized duties. The US had mobilized in a way never seen before.

◆ *see* US Passes the Selective Service Act p. 68

HITLER MEETS FRANCO (23 OCTOBER 1940)

The Spanish leader Francisco Franco offered his country's support to join the Axis Powers in June 1940, but the Germans showed little interest in his help at the time. On 23 October, Hitler finally agreed to meet Franco at Hendaye, near the Franco-Spanish border, and offered him the British-owned Gibraltar, but was not prepared to provide for the Spanish army or to ensure Franco a North African empire. As it transpired, Allied food and fuel kept Spain neutral and Franco only provided the Germans with submarine refuelling bases and other minor assistance.

PÉTAIN, HENRI-PHILLIPE (1856–1951)

Pétain's military career had almost come to an end by the outbreak of World War I, but he was persuaded to take command of French troops at Verdun. He was supremely efficient and in 1917 replaced Robert Nivelle as Commander-in-Chief. After the war he became a Field Marshall and was appointed War Minister in 1934. Pétain agreed to serve as the French Premier of Vichy France after the surrender of France in 1940. He signed an armistice with Germany and agreed to administer roughly 20 per cent of France, which would remain unoccupied by the Germans. He agreed to deport all Jews, maintain an army of 100,000 and actively prevent Frenchmen from joining the Allies. In addition, he would ensure that the French pay the costs of German occupation. Vichy troops, under Pétain's orders, resisted Allied actions in the Middle East and North Africa, but after the D-Day landings in June 1944 Pétain fled to Switzerland.

PÉTAIN MEETS HITLER (24 OCTOBER 1940)

The meeting between Hitler and French leader Pétain at Montoire on 24 October has been the subject of much controversy. Many claim that Pétain was trying to protect France from severe destruction until such time as Germany was defeated. He offered cooperation in return for peace and the retention of the French empire. Pétain also hoped that France could be transformed into a 'stable authoritarian order based on work, family, Fatherland'.

Pétain returned to France in April 1945 and was arrested for treason. He was tried and sentenced to death, but his venerable age and previous services to the French nation saved him from the hangman. He died in prison in 1951.

◆ see Henri-Phillipe Pétain p. 72

▲ *ABOVE: Hitler and Pétain meet to discuss the future of France.*

ITALY FAILS IN GREECE (28 OCTOBER 1940–1 MARCH 1941)

At 03:00 on 28 October 1940 the Italians delivered an ultimatum to the Greek government, demanding that Greece accept Italian occupation for the duration of the war in order to ensure Greek neutrality. The Greek Prime Minister Metaxas took this to be a declaration of war and at dawn the same day Italian troops crossed the Greek border. Greek resistance through early November continued and they began counterattacking. Lack of transport and armour prevented the Greeks from exploiting the

Italian weaknesses, but by January the Greeks had reached Albania. On 23 February the Greeks accepted Britain's offer of military assistance. Although seriously outnumbered, the Greeks were still making headway when, on 7 March, the first British troops began arriving at Piraeus. Seven days later the last Italian attempt at Greek submission failed.

◼ see British Arrive in Greece p. 88

▲ *ABOVE: Italian soldiers in Greece; the Italians failed in their attempts to suppress the Greeks, who were assisted by the arrival of British troops.*

ROOSEVELT IS RE-ELECTED (5 NOVEMBER 1940)

US President Roosevelt romped home to victory over his Republican rival Wendell Wilkie and became the first US President in the country's history to be re-elected for a third term. Roosevelt mustered 27 million votes to Wilkie's 22 million, although Roosevelt's share of the vote at 54.7 per cent was lower than his 1936 high of 60.8 per cent. Accusations describing Roosevelt as a dictator fell on deaf electoral ears.

◼ see Franklin D. Roosevelt p. 75

ROOSEVELT, FRANKLIN D. (1882–1945)

Roosevelt was born in New York and attended Harvard University and Colombia Law School; he married in 1905. His heart was set on a career in politics and he was elected to the New York Senate in 1910. President Woodrow Wilson appointed him Assistant Secretary of the Navy. He was nominated for Vice President in 1920 but in the summer of 1921 he was struck with an illness which temporarily cost him the use of his legs, but he was sufficiently recovered to attend the 1924 Democratic convention. In 1928 he became Governor of New York. Roosevelt became President in November 1932, serving the first of four terms. The US was in the middle of the Depression at the time, with 13 million people unemployed. In the first few days of his presidency, Roosevelt enacted a sweeping recovery programme which turned the country around. He adopted an isolationist policy but was firmly and implacably opposed to the Nazi regime and the intentions of Japan. He was a reluctant partner militarily but not materially prior to the attack on Pearl Harbor, but after this he mobilized the United States into an irresistible fighting machine. Roosevelt died before he could see the fruits of his victories, on 12 April 1945.

◆ see Lend-Lease Act p. 88

◀ LEFT: US President Franklin D. Roosevelt.

MOLOTOV, VYACHESLAV (1890–1986)

Molotov had been a colleague of Lenin, but after his death had switched allegiance to Stalin. He held several key positions until 1930, when Stalin appointed him Prime Minister. Stalin dismissed Maxim Litvino, his Commissar for Foreign Affairs in 1939 because of his Jewish ancestry, a subject causing difficulties in the ongoing discussions with Germany. Molotov replaced Litvino and signed the German-Russian Pact in Moscow (23 August 1939). Molotov received a telegram from the German Foreign Minister Joachim von Ribbentrop in September 1940, in which he was warned that Germany was about to join a pact with Italy and Japan. Molotov's spy network had already uncovered this information, and by December 1940 he had received advanced intelligence on the proposed German invasion of the Soviet Union.

Throughout the war Molotov remained at Stalin's side, attending all the conferences, including Yalta and Potsdam. Molotov lost his post in 1949, but after Stalin's death in 1953 he was reinstated. In 1956, Molotov joined the group that tried to oust Nikita Khrushchev and was demoted to a post in Mongolia. He was denounced in a purge and expelled from the Communist Party in 1964. Molotov died in Moscow in November 1986.

◆ *see* Tripartite Pact p. 70

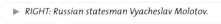

▶ *RIGHT: Russian statesman Vyacheslav Molotov.*

HITLER MEETS MOLOTOV (11 NOVEMBER 1940)

The meeting between Hitler and the Russian Foreign Minister, Vyacheslav Molotov, in November 1940 has often been cited as the reason why Germany turned on its erstwhile ally. Molotov was already intriguing in Romania and Hitler suspected that the Russians were behind the anti-German uprising in Yugoslavia. From this point Hitler paid close attention to the Russians, probably realizing conflict was inevitable.

TARANTO (11 NOVEMBER 1940)

By November 1940, the British Mediterranean Fleet was facing the task of defending a 3,220-km (2,000-mile) supply route from Gibraltar to Alexandria, via Malta. The obstacle was the powerful Italian fleet situated at Taranto.

At 20:40 on 11 November, the first of 12 Swordfish aircraft left HMS *Illustrious*, and arrived over Taranto at 22:56. Their first victim was the 29,000-ton battleship *Conte di Cavour*; two torpedoes hit the *Littorio*, while more aircraft tackled the Italian cruisers, destroyers and submarines. A second wave arrived over the harbour, claiming the *Caio Duillio*. For the loss of only two aircraft, the Italian fleet had been mauled; it fled for the safety of Naples harbour. Chillingly, the attack on Taranto became the blueprint for the Japanese attack on Pearl Harbor.

FLYING STRING BAGS (1936–45)

The Swordfish aircraft known as the Flying String Bag came into service with the Fleet Air Arm in 1936. Despite its World War I appearance, it outclassed all other aircraft that were developed to replace it and consequently stayed in service throughout the war. The aircraft was designed as a torpedo attack or reconnaissance aircraft. Some 2,391 were built and its most glorious moment during the war took place during the naval Battle of Taranto. Only 21 swordfish were involved in the sortie but they managed to destroy three battleships, a cruiser, two destroyers and other ancillary vessels.

see Sinking of the *Bismark* p. 107

BOMBING OF COVENTRY (14 NOVEMBER 1940)

During the night of 14 November, arguably the worst Luftwaffe air raid outside London took place when the British city of Coventry was carpet-bombed. The Germans intended to destroy the city's productive capacity, as even then it was the centre of the British automobile industry. After the attack, the Germans coined their own word, 'coventrisieren' which meant to annihilate, or raze to the ground. Some 449 German aircraft were involved in the raid, dropping around 600 tons of high explosives and thousands of incendiary bombs. By November the weekly death toll from German raids had fallen to 3,000 from a previous high of around 6,000. After the war, Coventry was twinned with the similarly devastated Dresden.

see German Rocket Programme p. 271

HUNGARY ENTERS THE WAR (20–23 NOVEMBER 1940)

On 20 November 1940 Count Teleki, the Hungarian Prime Minister, and his Foreign Minister, Count Casaky, signed the necessary documents linking Hungary to the German-Japanese-Italian Tripartite Pact. Effectively Hungary had joined the war. On 23 November Romania followed suit and the following day Slovakia became involved in the conflict. Hungary and Romania would provide Germany with much-needed manpower and industry.

see Germany Invades the Soviet Union p. 109

▶ RIGHT: The British city of Coventry was razed to the ground by the Luftwaffe.

BRITISH LAUNCH AN OFFENSIVE IN NORTH AFRICA (9 DECEMBER 1940)

After taking Sidi Barrani on 16 September 1940, the Italians took no further action. British commander Archibald Wavell began his offensive and broke through the lines with just two divisions against seven Italian formations. In just four days of fighting, four Italian divisions were obliterated and 38,000 prisoners taken. The haul included 1,000 trucks, over 70 tanks and 237 guns. By 12 December the only Italians remaining on Egyptian soil were prisoners. By 25 December the prisoner tally had reached 35,949. Continued attacks led to the fall of Bardia and another 40,000 prisoners. By 20 January Hitler had decided to send German troops to North Africa. The Italians continued to retreat towards Benghazi and a further 20,000 men were captured at Beda Fomm.

◆ see Archibald Wavell p. 80

WAVELL, ARCHIBALD (1883–1950)

By 1939 Wavell had already served in the Boer War and World War I (where he had lost his left eye). In July he was placed in command of the troops in the Middle East and in September his small force faced Graziani's attempt to capture Egypt. Wavell stopped them at Mersa Matruh, then in December launched a counteroffensive. Wavell's men pushed the Italians back some 500 km (311 miles), but by March 1941 Wavell faced Rommel, who forced the British out of Libya. Wavell attempted a counteroffensive in June 1941, but his attacks faltered at Halfaya Pass and Churchill replaced him with Auchinleck. Wavell was sent to Burma, but a lack of resources forced him to resign in February 1942. In January 1943, now a Field Marshall, Wavell again tried to force the Japanese out of Burma, but by spring of that year, his troops were being commanded in the field by Slim. Wavell became the Viceroy of Burma and was later replaced by Lord Mountbatten. He returned to

England in 1947 and became Lord Lieutenant of the County of London. Wavell wrote five books between 1928 and 1947, including campaign histories and theories of military tactics. He died in May 1950.

◆ *see* Allies Enter Libya and Capture Tobruk p. 84

▼ *BELOW: British commander Archibald Wavell.(right), with General O'Connor.*

1941

ALLIES ENTER LIBYA AND CAPTURE TOBRUK (5 JANUARY 1941)

Allied forces entered Libya on 5 January 1941 and British troops began attacking Tobruk on 21 January. After just a day the garrison surrendered and the British captured 30,000 prisoners, 70 tanks and 200 guns. By

1 February the Italians had abandoned Benghazi and on 6 February, after destroying 80 Italian tanks, the Australians led the entry into Benghazi and the British prepared for the battle of Beda Fomm.

◘ see Germans Launch an Offensive in North Africa p. 89

◄ LEFT: British troops and tanks wait to enter a burning Tobruk.

BATTLE OF BEDA FOMM (2 FEBRUARY 1941)

The Battle of Beda Fomm was a truly catastrophic Italian defeat that took place some 190 km (120 miles) south of Benghazi on the Libyan coast road. Advanced elements of the British 7th Armoured Division managed to cut across the desert and block the retreating Italian 10th Army. During the battle, in which the Italians were ambushed, some 25,000 prisoners, 100 tanks, 216 guns and 1,500 other vehicles were captured. The British offensive was over, with 500 dead, 55 missing and 1,373 wounded. Thirty-thousand British troops had advanced 800 km (500 miles) in two months, destroying 10 divisions and taking 130,000 captives, 400 tanks, and 1,290 guns. Graziani was relieved and replaced by Garibaldi, who dug in and awaited the drive on Tripoli – which never came.

▲ ABOVE: The British infantry tank Matilda.

MATILDA (1940–42)

The tank's bizarre appearance, which resembled a floating duck, acquired it the name of Matilda. The first versions were slow and new developments – including armoured skirting and thicker armour on the hull and turret – only added weight. A new version, called the Matilda Senior, was armed with 40-mm Vickers machine guns, instead of the earlier 7.7-mm or 12.7- mm. Twenty-three Matildas were available to the 7th Armoured Division when they were redeployed in France in May 1940. They proved effective and only very heavy German field howitzers or 88-mm anti-aircraft guns could penetrate their armour. After Dunkirk, Matilda IIs became the standard British infantry tank, used extensively in North Africa, Gazala (March 1942), and Tobruk. But gradually the Matilda tank was replaced by the Valentine.

ROMMEL TAKES COMMAND OF THE AFRIKA KORPS (12 FEBRUARY 1941)

Rommel arrived in Tripoli two days before the advanced guard of his Afrika Korps. He was given the task of rescuing the Italian forces that had suffered a series of defeats against the British in North Africa. As it transpired, the arrival of German forces stiffened Italian resolve and soon Rommel was forced on the offensive, taking his initiative from the British.

see Germans Launch an Offensive in North Africa p. 89

10,000 JEWS ARE DEPORTED FROM VIENNA (16 FEBRUARY 1941)

Around 10,000 Jews from Vienna and the surrounding area were earmarked for deportation under what was termed the Madagascar Plan. Deportation in the first 18 months of the war was the centrepiece of dealing with Jews as far as the Nazis were concerned. Indeed, in the Vienna area the pre-war Jewish population had been 166,000, 100,000 of whom emigrated before the war. The remainder were deported to concentration camps. After the invasion of Russia, it became clear that the means of dealing with Russian Jews (mobile firing squads) could not be used on western Jews and it was therefore decided that they should be deported to the east, where they would be killed in extermination camps.

see SS Begins Mass Murders p. 109

EXTERMINATION CAMPS BECOME OPERATIONAL (1 MARCH 1941)

The Germans constructed six concentration camps in Poland, the largest of which – Auschwitz-Brikenau – was officially opened on 1 March 1941. By the time it closed in 1944 1.4 million Jews had been murdered there. The system of deporting Jews to the six key extermination camps (Auschwitz-Brikenau, Auschwitz, Chelmno, Belzec, Sobibor and Treblink) became the standard method of dealing with Jews and these camps would account for 3.5 million lives. Belzec also came into operation in March 1941, Sobibor in April and Treblink in July.

Their existence was considered an utmost secret and only a handful of the prisoners ever managed to escape. These camps can be differentiated from the other concentration camps in that their sole purpose was for execution; they did not have facilities for slave labour.

◆ see Goering Presents the Final Solution p. 116

◀ LEFT: The infamous concentration camp at Auschwitz in Poland.

LEND-LEASE ACT (3 MARCH 1941)

On 3 March 1941 US Congress passed the necessary legislation to allow
President Roosevelt to sell, transfer, exchange or lend military equipment
to countries engaged in fighting against the Axis powers. Some 38
countries would be the beneficiaries of this aid, worth some $50 billion;
Britain would be the main borrower ($31 billion). The move had been
prompted by events in July 1940 when Britain had lost 11 destroyers in 10
days. Churchill had requested immediate assistance from Roosevelt and
the President responded by exchanging 50 destroyers for 99-year leases
on British bases in the Caribbean and Newfoundland. A major debate
erupted in the United States as to whether they should aid Britain or
maintain neutrality. Churchill had pleaded, 'Give us the tools and we'll
finish the job.'

see Atlantic Charter p. 116

BRITISH ARRIVE IN GREECE (7 MARCH 1941)

In response to the agreement with the Greeks, the British Expeditionary
Force began arriving at Piraeus and Volos on 7 March 1941. Britain had
promised 100,000 troops but in the event could only commit 57,000 or
four divisions, two of which were armoured. In the wake of the
successful British offensive against the Italians in North Africa, the
redeployment could not have come at a worse time; only a month
previously Rommel had taken command.

see Germany Invades Yugoslavia and Greece p. 92

YUGOSLAVIA ENTERS THE WAR (25 MARCH 1941)

On 19 March 1941 the Germans had issued an ultimatum to Yugoslavia
to allow them to pass through Yugoslav territory and join the Tripartite
Pact. In return they would be given Thessaloniki and parts of Greek

Macedonia. On 20 March Yugoslavia agreed in principle and despite a
British warning on 24 March, signed the Tripartite Act the following day
in Vienna, with Hitler, Ribbentrop and the Japanese Ambassador present.

see Germany Invades Yugoslavia and Greece p. 92

AXIS VESSELS ARE SEIZED (30 MARCH 1941)

On 27 March 1941 meetings in Washington between British and
American military advisors closed and a strategy was formed in the
event of the US entering the war. Three days later the United States,
Mexico, Costa Rica and Venezuela took all German, Italian and Danish
ships berthed in their harbours into protective custody. By this stage
the exchange of information between Britain and the US had reached
a wartime footing.

see Greenland is Placed Under US Control p. 93

GERMANS LAUNCH AN OFFENSIVE IN NORTH AFRICA (30 MARCH 1941)

Having spent a month in
North Africa, Rommel made
his first move on 24 March,
when he reoccupied El
Agheila, on the border
between Tripolitania and
Cyrenaica. He launched his
first counteroffensive six
days later, with a
combination of German
and Italian forces. They

▶ RIGHT: German tanks in Libya.

engaged British troops at Mersa Brega, forcing the British to withdraw, having lost 80 armoured vehicles. By 2 April Rommel had retaken Agedabia and Zuetina, forcing the British to evacuate Benghazi. Rommel's Afrika Korps was still under strength but he was facing a much-depleted British and Commonwealth force that had seen most of its experienced troops and commanders transferred to operations in Greece. Rommel would continue to advance on the shocked enemy.

◆ *see* Rommel's Afrika Korps p. 90

ROMMEL'S AFRIKA KORPS (1941–43)

Rommel's Afrika Korps came into existence in 1941 as the German contribution to the North African war effort. Throughout the war units including the 10th Panzer, 15th Panzer, 90th Light and 164th Light remained integral parts of the Afrika Korps. They were to accompany Rommel across the width of North Africa with his first offensive in April 1941, contend with the British operations Brevity and Battleaxe and then resume the offensive once more between late 1941 and 1942. Most of the units also fought during Operation Crusader, Alam el Halfa and resisted Montgomery during Lightfoot but were decisively defeated during Supercharge. They were then pursued across North Africa, only to discover that Allied forces had landed in Tunisia; many of them would fall into captivity by 1943. At the time of the surrender and the break-up of the Afrika Korps, Rommel was no longer in command. He had been replaced by General Von Arnim. Many of the units would continue to exist and some found themselves posted to the Eastern Front or back under Rommel's command, not as the Afrika Korps, but as mobile units positioned behind the main defence lines along the French or Belgian coasts, aiming to prevent Allied landings.

◆ *see* Erwin Rommel p. 149

GERMANS CAPTURE BENGHAZI AND BESIEGE TOBRUK (4–10 APRIL 1941)

British and Commonwealth troops, under orders to withdraw should they encounter any serious Axis opposition, began to retire eastwards, allowing Rommel to enter Benghazi. He continued to push forward from 4 April, capturing the British General O'Connor and General Neame, and taking Derna three days later. By 10 April Allied troops had withdrawn to Tobruk and were cut off from the rest of the army.

◆ *see* Renewed German Offensive and Gazala Line p. 148

▲ *ABOVE: The Germans enter Benghazi.*

GERMANY INVADES YUGOSLAVIA AND GREECE (6–16 APRIL 1941)

At 05:15 on 6 April German forces invaded Yugoslavia and Greece, attacking the former with no declaration of war. The attacks were supported by Hungarian and Italian units. The cause of the invasion had been the overthrow of the pro-German government in Yugoslavia and Hitler had moved quickly to eliminate the chance of Allied occupation. By 8 April the Yugoslav army was on the verge of collapse and the Germans were advancing on all fronts. Zagreb fell on 10 April, Nis and Skopjy had already fallen, denying the Greeks or the British the opportunity of assisting the Yugoslavs. Belgrade fell on 12 April and by 17 April the Yugoslavian army had been destroyed and the last centre of resistance in Bosnia had collapsed. More than 300,000 prisoners had been taken.

◧ see Yugoslavia and Greece Surrender p. 94

▼ BELOW: German troops advancing through Serbia, Yugoslavia, after the invasion.

JASENOVAC (1941–1945)

Jasenovac was a concentration-camp complex established some 100 km (62 miles) south of Zagreb. Unlike the other camps, it was set up and administered by the pro-German Croatians. Jasenovac, dubbed 'the Auschwitz of the Balkans' was run by feared Ustaska security police. Various estimates have been made of the number of Serbs, Jews and gypsies murdered at Jasenovac, but it was certainly no less than 85,000. This was just one part of the overall genocide in Yugoslavia as at least 600,000 Serbs were murdered by the regime (around a third of the pre-war Serb population). The camps were liberated by Tito's partisans in April 1945; few came to trial for their crimes.

GREENLAND PLACED UNDER US CONTROL (10 APRIL 1941)

Having reached an agreement with the Danish government, US troops began occupying Greenland as part of the US policy to deny the Germans the North Atlantic and to protect the ever-growing numbers of convoys carrying war supplies to Britain. The Atlantic Fleet Support Group of the US navy began operating out of Greenland in order to deal with the growing threat of the German navy.

◆ *see* Roosevelt Orders the Freezing of German Assets p. 108

SOVIET-JAPANESE NON-AGGRESSION PACT SIGNED (13 APRIL 1941)

The Japanese Foreign Minister Matsuoko – having met Hitler in Berlin on 4 April, where they discussed the possibility of an attack on Singapore and an impending conflict with the US – moved on to Moscow on 13 April. Here he signed a five-year non-aggression treaty with the Russian Foreign Minister, Molotov. Japan was putting in place the last pieces of the jigsaw of support and neutrality they needed.

◆ *see* Soviets Denounce the Pact with Japan p. 284

YUGOSLAVIA AND GREECE SURRENDER (17–23 APRIL 1941)

Yugoslavia officially surrendered on 17 April 1941 and on the following day German troops pushed past Mount Olympus, threatening to cut off British troops. Meanwhile Italian and other German troops broke through Greek lines and by 20 April they were surrounded. Officially Greek resistance ended the following day, when 16 divisions surrendered. Two days later, for the cameras – and on Hitler's orders – the Greek surrender was repeated near Thessaloniki.

▶ see Athens Falls p. 96

◀ *LEFT: German tanks in Athens.*

▲ ABOVE: Troops completing a bridge after the capture of Baghdad.

BRITAIN LAUNCHES OFFENSIVE AND CAPTURES BAGHDAD
(17 APRIL–1 JUNE 1941)

On 4 April 1941, the pro-German Rashid Ali seized control in Iraq. On 17 April British troops crossed the border and on 2 May they clashed with Iraqi troops at Habbaniyah; within two days they had occupied Bazra. By the end of the month Baghdad was surrounded and Rashid Ali surrendered (replaced by Emi Abdullah). British troops entered Baghdad the following day, securing this strategically important region.

◄ see British Occupy Syria and Enter Iran with Soviets p. 114

ATHENS FALLS (27 APRIL 1941)

Despite the Greek surrender, many units continued to fight alongside the British. German paratroops began landing on Greek islands on 24 April and two days later they captured Corinth on the mainland. British troops continued their retreat, embarking from several Greek ports. Athens fell on April 27 and the last British troops left the following day, bound for Crete, leaving nearly 13,000 men behind.

see Battle for Crete p. 106

STALIN BECOMES PREMIER OF THE SOVIET UNION (6 MAY 1941)

On 6 May 1941 the Russian Praesidium of the Supreme Soviet nominated Joseph Stalin to become President of the Council of People's Commissars. Stalin already held the rank of Communist Party Secretary and in this deft manoeuvre he was able to secure even more power. He was now better able to enforce his own policies and visions of Russia, its future and its strength and power.

see Joseph Stalin p. 113

RAF LAUNCHES A BOMBER OFFENSIVE ON GERMANY (8 MAY 1941)

On 7 May 1941 the Germans heavily bombed the Humber area of Britain; the following night, in retaliation, British bombers carried out a massive raid on Hamburg. The same night German bombers were back over the Humber region and also made attacks on London. On 9 May the RAF hit Bremen but the following evening a number of key targets in London were hit.

BOMBER COMMAND (1936–68)

Bomber Command was formed on 14 July 1936 at High Wycombe in Buckinghamshire and was formally disbanded on 30 April 1968. It has been estimated that between 3 September 1939 and 8 August 1945 RAF

▲ ABOVE: The result of the British bombing raid on Hamburg.

Bomber Command flew some 387,416 sorties, dropped 955,000 tons of
bombs and lost 8,953 aircraft and 55,573 personnel. A wide variety of
airmen from different countries, including Australia, New Zealand,
Canada, South Africa and Rhodesia (Zimbabwe) flew with Bomber
Command during the war years. Typically, a crew member would serve a
tour of duty of 30 operations. Mathematically it was nearly impossible to
survive this number of missions, yet many did. Bomber Command
initially used aircraft such as the Wellington, the Hampden, the Blenheim
and the Whitley. Undoubtedly the most famous of the heavy bombers
used was the Lancaster (the other two were the Manchester and the
Stirling). It was the Lancaster that was used on the famous Dambuster
raid. The Halifax came into operation in 1944 and was considered to be
one of the finest of their aircraft. Bomber Command hit enemy-occupied
targets across the length and breadth of Europe throughout the war. The
last attack took place on 24 April 1945.

◆ see Arthur 'Bomber' Harris p. 98

HARRIS, ARTHUR 'BOMBER' (1892–1984)

Harris was a former mine owner and tobacco planter in Rhodesia (Zimbabwe), joining the Rhodesian regiment in campaigns during World War I in south-west Africa. By 1915, Harris had joined the Royal Flying Corps and the following year took command of 44 Squadron. In the interwar years, he served in India, Iran and Iraq, but by 1939, with the rank of Air Vice Marshal, he had been assigned to Bomber Command. In February 1942 Harris took over Bomber Command and developed the concept of area bombing (blanket bombing). He was severely criticized for this tactic, but Harris argued that the attacks on Hamburg, Cologne and Dresden were intended to break German civilian morale. Indeed, some six million homes were either destroyed or damaged and 600,000 civilians killed in the raids.

In 1942, however, he did assist in the formation of the Pathfinders, an attempt to ease the transition to precision bombing. By the end of the war, nearly 60,000 Bomber Command crew had been lost. In 1946 Harris became Marshall of the Royal Air Force, but retired soon after to write his memoirs. He immigrated to South Africa and died in April 1984.

◼ see British Launch their Largest Air Operation p. 128

◀ LEFT: 'Bomber' Harris.

HESS, RUDOLF (1894–1987)

Rudolf Hess was born in Egypt, but moved to Germany before World War I, where he served as an infantryman and pilot (twice wounded) then joined the Freikorps, a right-wing paramilitary group which put down Communist revolts in Germany.

Joining the Nazi party in 1920, Hess became a strong-arm brawler for Hitler against the Communists. Hess was imprisoned for his involvement in the Munich Beer Hall Putsch (1923), but returned to the party after release in 1925. After the Nazis came to power in 1932, Hess became Deputy Führer. Despite this, Hess was often left out of the decision-making, and he gradually became more isolated from Hitler.

On 10 May 1941 Hess navigated an aircraft across the North Sea and landed within 30 miles of the Duke of Hamilton in

▲ ABOVE: Rudolph Hess.

Scotland, who he had met at the Berlin Olympics in 1936. Hess desired to secure peace with Great Britain and presented his British captors with a peace proposal; Hitler disowned him and the British dismissed his offers. Hess remained in prison throughout the war, coming to trial at Nuremberg; although it was clear he was mentally unwell he was sentenced to life imprisonment. He committed suicide in prison at the age of 92 years.

◪ see The Secret War p. 100

HESS FLIES TO SCOTLAND (10 MAY 1941)

Rudolf Hess parachuted from a Me110 into the village of Eaglesham, near Glasgow to deliver a peace plan to the Duke of Hamilton, whom he had met at the 1936 Berlin Olympic Games. Once it became clear that Hess was not speaking on behalf of Hitler, Churchill dismissed any suggestions of peace. The Germans claimed that he had been suffering from hallucinations and was mentally disordered. Hess was imprisoned in Buchanan Castle, the Tower of London and then in Abergavenny. At the time Hess's arrival was a sensation as it pointed to dissention within the ranks of the Nazi Party.

◘ *see* Rudolf Hess p. 99

THE SECRET WAR (1939–45)

The desire to be appraised of exactly what the enemy was doing reached incredible heights during the war. In Britain, MI5 and MI6 were inextricably involved, but there were dozens of other smaller organizations committing espionage, undertaking covert operations and using new communications technology. There was also the fascinating world of codes and ciphers, in which both sides attempted to ensure that their most secret information and orders were not compromised by the enemy. Many of the techniques picked up by various operatives would subsequently be used during the Cold War. Equally as fascinating were the various Special Forces which fought a semi-covert war, at least in as much as they were primarily designed as information gatherers, kidnappers or raiders. Britain had its own Special Air Service and Long Range Desert Group, and across occupied Europe there were members of the Special Operations Executive guiding foreign nationals against the enemy. There was a clandestine world that pitted itself against the Gestapo and the Abwehr. Perhaps the best-kept secret of the war was the development of the atomic bombs in the US, known as the Manhattan Project.

BLETCHLEY PARK (1939–45)

In the summer of 1939, a group of scholars recruited as code-breakers arrived at Bletchley Park. Their mission was to break the German Enigma cipher, considered to be an unbreakable code. The odds against them were a staggering 150,000,000,000,000,000,000:1. The team built Colossus, the world's first computer, to crack the code used by the German military. The work at Bletchley Park has been said to have shortened the war by at least two years. At the height of the operations at Bletchley Park, 10,000 people were engaged in deciphering German codes. Everything was carried out in secrecy, Churchill himself saying of those there that they were 'the geese that laid the golden eggs and never cackled'.

see The Secret War p. 100

▼ BELOW: *Bletchley Park, where the Enigma code was finally cracked.*

ENIGMA (1918–45)

The German Enigma machine was invented in 1918 and was originally used for secured banking communications. A letter could be typed into a machine which sent electrical impulses through a series of rotating

wheels, contacts and wires to produce the ciphered letter. The machine operator who received the message would have to type in the code and then see the deciphered message light up letter by letter on the keyboard. Polish intelligence had broken the code in 1932 and prior to September 1939 the cipher was only changed once every few months. German operator mistakes and the acquisition of an Enigma machine finally allowed the decryption teams, led by Alan Turing, to break the code. Intercept stations collected German radio traffic which was decoded and then sent to the military.

◆ see Second Battle of El Alamein p. 181

▲ ABOVE: Enigma machine.

CHETNIKS BEGIN RESISTANCE AGAINST THE GERMANS (10 MAY 1941)

The Chetniks were Serbian royalists who formed guerrilla groups to resist Axis occupation and the pro-German Croatian government. They were led by Draza Mihailovic, and their desire was to liberate Yugoslavia and restore the monarchy. The Chetnik base was at Ravna Gora and for them and Tito's Partisans in the early months it was very much a question of survival; both struggled to win support.

◆ see Chetniks Battle with Tito p. 128

LAST MAJOR GERMAN ATTACK ON LONDON (10 MAY 1941)

After nine months of the Blitz, 550 Luftwaffe aircraft dropped hundreds of high explosive and an estimated 100,000 incendiaries on London. Civilian casualties were estimated at around 1,400, making this the biggest German raid since the beginning of the war. The RAF accounted for 29 German aircraft and it seemed that the damage to civilian homes, the Houses of Parliament, Westminster Abbey, St Paul's Cathedral and the British Museum was the beginning of a new phase. In fact this turned out to be the last major raid on London. The high point of the Luftwaffe attempt to crush Britain had now passed. In all an estimated 20,000 Londoners were killed and 25,000 injured during the war.

◄► *see* Blitz Begins p. 66

▼ *BELOW: St Paul's Cathedral in London stands among smoking ruins.*

LUFTWAFFE (1935–45)

The German Luftwaffe was created in May 1935, following the denunciation of the Treaty of Versailles. The 100,000-man Reichswehr became the Wehrmacht and consisted of an army, a navy and an air force. Between 1939 and 1945 3.4 million Germans served in the Luftwaffe. Of these an estimated 165,000 were killed, 155,000 missing and 192,000 wounded. The Luftwaffe not only consisted of the air units,

but also parachutists, conventional field divisions, the elite Hermann Goering Division and thousands of smaller units, such as engineers and anti-aircraft personnel. Training had taken place in secret in Russia and its pilots were some of the best to fly in the war. Of the 7,361 men awarded the highest German honour, the Knight's Cross, 1,785 were from the Luftwaffe.

◘ *see* Luftwaffe Bombs Moscow p. 115

BATTLE OF THE ATLANTIC (1940–1945)

The Atlantic Ocean was a major theatre of operations during World War II. From the opening day of the war the German navy sought to cut off Europe from the United States and its other trading partners. Indeed by 1 October 1939 they had already sunk 153,000 tons of merchant shipping. In 1940 Britain needed 120,000 tons of food and fuel each day in order to survive. This pressure became increasingly intense after the fall of mainland Europe. When the US first entered the war they had little success against the German navy; U-boats were being delivered at a rate of 30 each month and in June the Allies lost 173 ships. By March 1943 400 U-boats were in action, but March proved to be the turning point and by July the Allies were sinking German ships faster than they could build them, while the Germans were sinking less than the Americans could construct. By the time the Germans surrendered in May 1945, U-boats had sunk 3,500 merchant ships, nearly 2,500 of which were in the North Atlantic. This amounted to 18,300,000 tons (including 175 war ships). A full three-quarters of the German U-boats had also been lost.

◘ *see* Wolf Packs p. 26

◀ *LEFT: A German Luftwaffe pilot with his Stuka plane.*

BATTLE FOR CRETE (20–31 MAY 1941)

The island of Crete, strategically positioned in the eastern Mediterranean, had assumed importance by the middle of 1941 due to its position midway between Europe and Egypt. Possession was vital for the struggle for North Africa. After air raids on the morning of 20 May, German gliders and parachutists dropped on the west of the island, around Malme airfield and Chania, both crucial to the Germans for reinforcements. By the end of the day the airfield and the city were still in Allied hands and German casualties were mounting.

Overnight the Royal Navy intercepted German and Italian shipping en route to the island. By morning the British fleet had been driven off by the Luftwaffe. Despite heavy pressure, German troops secured Malme and reinforcements poured in, allowing the capture of Chania and the anchorage of Suda Bay. The Germans now pushed along the north coast to the capital, Heraklion and the remnants of the Allies fought their way to Sphakia on the south coast for evacuation. Of the 22,000 Germans committed to Operation Merkur, 6,000 had been lost. Allied strength, in excess of 41,000 had dwindled to the 15,000 that had been evacuated to Egypt.

SINKING OF THE HMS *HOOD* (24 MAY 1941)

During the pursuit of the German ships *Bismark* and *Prinz Eugen* the *Hood* and the *Prince of Wales* engaged the enemy ships at a distance of 27 km (17 miles) to the east of Iceland. After an exchange of fire, a shell from the *Bismark* penetrated the *Hood*'s superstructure and exploded in the ammunition lockers. The *Hood* sank in minutes, claiming all but three of the 1,419-man crew. The *Prince of Wales* was also hit and prudently decided to withdraw, while the two German vessels broke away and sailed south.

⬧ *see* Sinking of the HMS *Ark Royal* p. 131

SINKING OF THE *BISMARK* (27 MAY 1941)

The German battleship *Bismark*, accompanied by the *Prinz Eugen* slipped out of the Baltic on 18 May 1941 and headed for the Atlantic. By 20 May the ships had reached the North Sea, but on the following day they were spotted by British reconnaissance aircraft. The whole fleet at Scapa Flow was mobilized to intercept them. The German ships were in Bergen, Norway when the HMS *Hood* and HMS *Prince of Wales*, accompanied by cruisers, left Scapa Flow. By 23 May the Germans had rounded Iceland when they were intercepted by the British. Just after dawn the following morning, after exchanging fire, the *Hood* was sunk with nearly all hands. Shortly after this the German ships disappeared and it was not until 26 May that they were found again, 1,126 km (700 miles) west of Brest. At 19:50 torpedoes from aircraft of the *Ark Royal* crippled the Bismark and the British surface fleet closed in for the kill. At 10:40 on 27 May, after being pulverized by the British fleet, the *Bismark* capsized and sank; only 110 of its crew of 2,300 men survived.

◆ *see* Battle of the Atlantic p. 105

▼ BELOW: The famous German battleship Bismark *sinks.*

ROOSEVELT ORDERS THE FREEZING OF GERMAN ASSETS (14 JUNE 1941)

Continuing pressure on the Axis powers without making an outright commitment to war, Roosevelt froze all German and Italian assets in the United States on 14 June 1941. Two days later the President closed the German Embassy and propaganda offices in the US. In retaliation, on 19 June, Germany and Italy asked the US to close their consulates in their respective countries. On 4 July Roosevelt told the nation that the US was heading for war.

see US and Britain Warn Japan p. 116

OPERATION BATTLEAXE FAILS TO RELIEVE TOBRUK (15 JUNE 1941)

Operation Battleaxe sought to reduce the pressure on Tobruk and relieve the fortress. Initially the British attacks were successful, but by the evening of 15 June German artillery fire had wreaked havoc on the Allied tanks. Rommel responded aggressively and launched counterattacks on the British and to avoid being cut off, the Allied troops retired to the Libyan-Egyptian border. Operation Battleaxe was over in just two days, prompting Churchill to replace Wavell with Auchinleck.

see Operation Crusader p. 131

INVASION OF MALTA PLANNED (21 JUNE 1941)

In discussions with Hitler on 21 June 1941, Mussolini agreed to postpone Operation Hercules, the planned invasion of Malta. He agreed to support Rommel's invasion of Egypt before tackling Malta. The proposal was to land three Italian parachute battalions and a German parachute division on Malta, supported by German and Italian aircraft. It was felt that the capture of the strategic point in the Mediterranean would disrupt convoys heading for North Africa.

see Malta VC p. 159

GERMANY INVADES THE SOVIET UNION (22 JUNE 1941)

At approximately 04:00 on 22 June 1941, the lead elements of over 100 German divisions began crossing into Russian-held territory. The total German strength amounted to almost 3.2 million men and 3,580 tanks. Around 2.5 million Russians would face them. The Germans advanced on five fronts, from the Baltic to the Black Sea. They opposition they met was ineffective and they were soon deep in Russian territory, having surrounded tens of thousands of Russian troops.

see Germans Drive East p. 111

▲ *ABOVE: German tanks enter Russia.*

SS BEGINS MASS MURDERS (JUNE 1941)

Much of the implementation of the Final Solution was carried out by the organization known as Einsatzgruppen, but the extermination-camp structure and management was overseen by members of the SS. The concentration camps were also used to provide slave labour for SS economic enterprises. Many of the concentration camps had come under the direct jurisdiction of the SS by the middle of 1941, as had the extermination camps. By the end of 1941 concentration camps contained

60,000 prisoners but from 1942 the increased numbers being sent to the camps and the sizes of the camps themselves grew enormously. By January 1945 the SS registered the figure of 741,211 in the concentration camps alone. The SS dictated every action in all the camps which had to be followed.

◈ *see* Goerring Presents the Final Solution p. 116

SECOND FINNISH–SOVIET WAR (25 JUNE 1941–4 SEPTEMBER 1944)

Following the German invasion of Russia, the Finns aimed to recapture the areas they had lost during the Winter War. This period was known to the Finns as the War of Continuation; from 25 June 1941 they sought to take up more favourable defensive positions and refused to cooperate with the Germans on the attacks on Leningrad. Border skirmishing continued through to the summer of 1944, by which time it had become clear that Germany was losing the war. The Russians attempted to level Helsinki in February 1944 by bombing, but launched their ground attack on 9 June. They penetrated the Finnish defences the following day and

▼ *BELOW: Finnish troops shelter behind smoking debris on the Karelian Front.*

the Finns retreated back to a second line of defence. A large battle took place in the Tali-Ihantala area (25 June–6 July), but Russian losses caused them to break off the attack. Meanwhile, other major Russian assaults continued until 11 July. The ceasefire was officially signed at 07:00 on 4 September 1944. The Russians only retained the area they had won during the Winter War. Finland had maintained its independence and much of its territorial integrity.

◆ see Winter War p. 27

▲ ABOVE: German tanks advancing across Russia.

GERMANS DRIVE EAST (28 JUNE 1941)

With German troops threatening Minsk and closing on Kiev towards the end of June 1940, the Russian army was either in full retreat or had already been cut off. By 9 July the Russians had lost over 300,000 men and 2,500 tanks; in the Bialystok sector, 40 divisions had been wiped out. German units began moving towards Smolensk, en route for Moscow. Elsewhere, the Germans and their allies were advancing on a broad front.

◆ see Stalin Begins a Scorched-Earth Policy p. 112

STALIN BEGINS A SCORCHED-EARTH POLICY (3 JULY 1941)

On 3 July 1941, for the first time since the invasion, Stalin addressed the Russian people, admitting vast losses of men and territory. He urged the Russians to resist until the bitter end and leave nothing for the Germans. He advocated a scorched-earth policy, in which everything of value that had to be left behind would be destroyed. He went on to say 'Military tribunals will pass summary judgement on any who fail in our defence, whether through panic or treachery, regardless of their position or rank. All efforts of the people must be exerted to beat the enemy. On to victory!' In response, all men between the ages of 16 and 60 were called up and given orders to defend positions to the last man at all costs.

◆ *see* Joseph Stalin p. 113

▼ *BELOW: A Russian town smoking as the Soviets retreat from the advancing Germans.*

STALIN, JOSEPH (1879–1953)

Stalin had worked his way towards leadership of the Communist Party in Russia by ordering the murder of all other leading figures associated with the Russian Revolution. He was to maintain his grip on Russia by mass arrests, death sentences and exile in Siberian labour camps during a succession of purges. In 1937 he began a series of purges in the Red Army and by 1939 he had liquidated nearly all the higher ranking officers. In 1939 he signed a non-aggression pact with Hitler, agreeing their spheres of influence in Eastern Europe, including the division of Poland. His invasion of Finland proved disastrous and when the Germans launched Operation Barbarossa (June 1941) the incompetence of the Red Army allowed the Germans to overrun western Russia, reaching the gates of Moscow. The entry of the United States in late 1941 provided the Russians with much-needed war material. It was his commander Zhukov's military skills that ultimately saved Russia. Stalin was still in place in the aftermath of the war and moulded much of eastern Europe in his vision of a Communist state.

◆ see Germans Cross the Dniepr p. 114

▲ ABOVE: Soviet leader Joseph Stalin, who ruled through fear and oppression.

BRITISH OCCUPY SYRIA AND ENTER IRAN WITH SOVIETS (14 JULY–29 AUGUST 1941)

In Syria an armistice was signed between the British and the French and Syria was declared independent. On 15 July British troops entered Beirut and Syria and Lebanon came under Allied control. On 26 August British troops occupied the oil fields at Abadan in Iran and the following day a new government was formed, allowing British and Russian troops to be stationed around the country.

◄ LEFT: British prisoners-of-war being returned after the occupation of Syria in 1941.

GERMANS CROSS THE DNIEPR (17 JULY 1941)

The Germans established a bridgehead near Mogilef on the River Dniepr, to the east of Minsk on 17 July 1941. Stalin's eldest son, serving as an artillery lieutenant, was captured near Vitebsk. By 27 July Smolensk was surrounded; more than 700,000 Russians had been trapped and 300,000 were taken prisoner along with 3,000 tanks and 1,000 aircraft. The German targets would now be the Crimea, Kharkov and the Donetz coal fields.

◄► see Germans Capture Novgorod p. 118

LUFTWAFFE BOMBS MOSCOW (21 JULY 1941)

With German troops continuing to advance on all fronts, Moscow fell within enemy reach. On the night of 21 July, massive night air attacks rained bombs on the Russian capital. Each day thousands more Russian troops fell into German hands as town after town was overrun. The Germans bombed Moscow again on 3 August and over 300,000 Russians surrendered near Smolensk two days later.

◆ see Hermann Goering p. 58

JAPANESE OCCUPY FRENCH INDO-CHINA (24 JULY 1941)

Japanese forces began occupying French-held Indo-China on 24 July 1941. Officially they were to collaborate with the French forces in its defence. The next day Japanese assets in Britain and the US were frozen; Japan reciprocated and Canada also froze their trade with Japan. By 29 July the Japanese occupation of Indo-China was complete. Britain sent reinforcements to Singapore on 6 August.

◆ see Tojo Becomes Prime Minister of Japan p. 121

▶ RIGHT: Japanese war planes.

GOERING PRESENTS THE FINAL SOLUTION (31 JULY 1941)

There had been ongoing discussions regarding the German's 'Jewish problem'. Much of the organization and planning had been left to Adolf Eichmann, who had been placed in charge of Jewish emigration. In 1941 he was appointed Head of the Gestapo, the department responsible for what they called the 'Final Solution'. Goering signed Eichmann's draft and charged Heydrich with the task of 'evacuating' all European Jews. Typically, the wording of the agreement was ambiguous, but everyone around the conference table knew what these carefully couched terms actually meant. Eichmann himself was interned by US troops in 1945, but escaped to South America. The Israelis discovered him in Argentina and in controversial circumstances brought him back to be tried in Jerusalem; he was hanged in May 1962.

see Jews Ordered to Wear Yellow Stars p. 118

US AND BRITAIN WARN JAPAN (6 AUGUST 1941)

On 26 July 1941 Roosevelt froze Japanese assets in the US, suspended trade, and set an oil embargo. On 6 August, along with the British, he warned the Japanese not to invade Thailand. Japan responded by stating it had no aggressive intentions. On 8 August the Japanese Ambassador to Washington proposed talks between Roosevelt and the Japanese Prime Minister to sort out differences between their countries.

see Atlantic Charter p. 116

ATLANTIC CHARTER (9–12 AUGUST 1941)

On 9 August 1941 British Prime Minister Churchill and US President Roosevelt met in Placentia Bay in Newfoundland and the following day opened the Atlantic Conference. The result of this conference – the Atlantic Charter – would define the war aims. Churchill wanted the US

▲ ABOVE: *A still from the film* Carve her name with pride, *showing how Goering's Final Solution involved the enslavement and execution of minority groups.*

to enter the war, but Roosevelt refused to make any guarantee of this. The two leaders agreed to give the Japanese a warning which stated 'Any further Japanese expansion would lead to a situation in which the government of the United States would see itself obliged to take counter-measures, even if that led to war.' Neither Roosevelt nor Churchill was under any illusions about Japanese intentions and they proposed to force the Japanese to accept that Thailand and French Indo-China should be neutral. Other issues were discussed and the conference broke up on 12 August.

⬦ *see* Creation of the United Nations p. 144

GERMANS CAPTURE NOVGOROD (17 AUGUST 1941)

In the northern sector of the Eastern Front, the Germans to the south-east of the key Russian city of Leningrad captured Novgorod on 17 August. In the south they took Dniepr and threatened Kharkov; the Crimea and Odessa were also surrounded. By 22 August the Russians had lost 1.25 million men, 14,000 tanks, 15,000 guns and over 11,000 aircraft. Between 24 and 26 August limited Russian counterattacks were defeated.

JEWS ORDERED TO WEAR YELLOW STARS (SEPTEMBER 1941)

The compulsory wearing of a yellow star to indicate that an individual was Jewish began in September 1941, in occupied Eastern Europe. The system was extended to the rest of the Third Reich territories shortly afterwards and all Jews over the age of six were obliged to wear one. The star had to be worn on the left side of all outer garments and was permanently stitched so that it could not easily be removed. The order was just another step in the Nazi Final Solution.

⬦ *see* Germans Murder 30,000 Jews at Kiev p. 121

LENINGRAD IS SURROUNDED (1 SEPTEMBER 1941)

German troops reached the southern shore of Lake Ladoga on
1 September 1941, cutting off the key city of Leningrad from the
rest of Russia. The Germans also established bridgeheads on the
Gulf of Finland. For 90 days German troops launched a series of
offensives all driving towards the capture of Leningrad. Although
the situation was desperate for the Russians, in an act of courageous
defiance, Zhukov ordered the city to be fortified – house by house,
street by street – to deny the Germans their prize.

◆ *see* Siege of Leningrad p. 120

▲ *ABOVE: The Siege of Leningrad.*

SIEGE OF LENINGRAD (8 SEPTEMBER 1941–27 JANUARY 1944)

The Siege of Leningrad officially began on 8 September 1941; it lasted until 27 January 1944, making it the longest siege in the war. Nearly three million Russian civilians were trapped in the city for the duration of the siege. Food and fuel were in limited supply and by the winter of 1941 there was no heating or water. By January 1942 daily rations had dropped to just 125 g of bread per day and from January to February an estimated 200,000 people died of starvation or the cold alone. Despite the hardships, however, the people of Leningrad held out with remarkable tenacity.

The siege was officially broken in January 1943, but it was not for another year that it was fully lifted. By this time between 650,000 and 800,000 Leningrad citizens and soldiers had been killed. Some half a million of these are buried in the Piskariovskoye Memorial Cemetery. The Russians made it a national task to restore Leningrad to its former glory after the many months of constant bombardment. War damage had affected virtually every building, yet Leningrad – now called St Petersburg – was successfully restored and museums and public buildings reopened.

see Germans Capture Kharkov and Kursk p. 122

ROOSEVELT ORDERS A 'SHOOT-FIRST' POLICY (11 SEPTEMBER 1941)

On 4 September the USS *Greer* was attacked by a German U-boat in the waters south-west of Iceland. Roosevelt was furious and on 11 September ordered a 'shoot-first' policy to all US ships encountering either German or Italian vessels. Any ship that threatened the passage of US merchant ships or their escorts would henceforth come under attack from the US navy. The policy was to take immediate effect.

see Sinking of the USS *Reuben James* p. 122

2

GERMANS MURDER 30,000 JEWS AT KIEV (28–29 SEPTEMBER 1941)

German Special Operations squads, known as 'Einsatzgruppen', entered
both Poland and Russia behind the advancing German armies with the
specific purpose of rounding up and killing Jews. At Kiev, in a ravine
known as Babi Yar to the north-west, 30,000 Jews were murdered in just
two days. Many had been turned in by local Ukrainians.

see First Jews Gassed p. 138

TOJO BECOMES PRIME MINISTER OF JAPAN (17 OCTOBER 1941)

Tojo replaced Konoye as the Japanese Prime Minister. The new leader
symbolized the pro-war faction in Japan; it would be at his insistence
that Japan went to war against the Allies and, significantly, the US.
As a politician, he refused to meddle in operational matters, but was
a capable bureaucrat who was more than able to carry out the wishes
of the Japanese Imperial Cabinet. Throughout the war he isolated
Yamashita, possibly one of the most talented Japanese commanders, due
to a personal dislike. Tojo accepted responsibility for Japanese reversals
and when Saipan was lost in July 1944 he resigned, blaming himself.

see Hideki Tojo p. 121

TOJO, HIDEKI (1884–1948)

Considered by many to be one of the principal architects of Japanese
involvement in the war, Tojo had rapidly risen through the military ranks
throughout the 1930s. His career breakthrough occurred in May 1938
when the then-Prime Minister, Fumimaro Kondoye, appointed him to
the post of Vice Minister of War. When Kondoye's government fell, he
returned to the army as commander of the air forces.

In the years leading up to the Japanese attack on Pearl Harbor, Tojo
had supported an aggressive foreign policy, arguing that pre-emptive

attacks on China and Russia were the only way to ensure Japan's long term prospects. It was Tojo who ordered the attack on Pearl Harbor on 7 December 1941, when a negotiated settlement with the US seemed doomed to failure.

Tojo held a number of civilian and military posts, including that of Prime Minister until early 1944, when he became Commander-in-Chief of the General Staff. He resigned after the fall of Saipan in July 1944. He was captured by US forces after a bungled attempt to commit suicide, tried as a war criminal, found guilty and executed on 23 December 1948.

◆ *see* Japanese Capture Kuala Lumpur p. 146

GERMANS CAPTURE KHARKOV AND KURSK (24 OCTOBER–3 NOVEMBER 1941)

By 20 October 1941, the Germans were within 65 miles of Moscow. Three days later two German armies were closing in on Kharkov. As bad weather began to hinder the offensive against Moscow, Kharkov was taken on 24 October. After seizing most of the Crimea in the south, the Germans captured Kursk to the north of Kharkov on 3 November before continuing their march on Moscow.

◆ *see* Germans Capture Rostov and Launch an Assault on Moscow p. 132

SINKING OF THE USS *REUBEN JAMES* (31 OCTOBER 1941)

The USS *Reuben James* was part of an escort force protecting shipping bound for Britain, one of five destroyers assigned to convoy HX-156. At around 05:25 on 31 October, the *Reuben James* was torpedoed by the U-Boat U-522. The torpedo hit the ship's magazine and it sank in minutes, claiming 100 of the crew and becoming the first US vessel lost to hostile action.

◆ *see* Allies Declare War on Japan p. 137

WAR IN CHINA (1931–45)

The Japanese invaded north-eastern China in 1931. Over the 15 years of war that ensued, some 30 million Chinese would be killed. The Japanese were unable to agree terms with the Chinese and there was little attempt to do so. Indeed, the Japanese policy seemed to revolve around mass reprisal killings, slave labour and other violent indignities against the civilian population. The infamous Rape of Nanking involved the slaughter of civilians that lasted for a staggering six weeks and claimed the lives of over 300,000 people. Even after the war ended, China would be so torn that the Chinese Nationalists and Chinese Communists would never come to terms. In recent years it has also been alleged that the Japanese systematically used biological or germ warfare and that they deliberately spread diseased rats in several areas of China, which could

▼ *BELOW: Japanese tanks breach a fjord in China.*

have claimed as many as 20,000 lives. During the war, US and British forces supported and supplied the Chinese. Ultimately, however, the war sapped the strength of the nationalist government and was a contributing factor in the Communist victory in 1949.

◆ see Flying Tigers p. 124

▲ ABOVE: Japanese troops in China.

FLYING TIGERS (1941–45)

The volunteer group Flying Tigers, was the brainchild of former US Army Air Corps Colonel, Claire L. Chennault. As Air Advisor to the Chinese nationalist government, he discovered that the Chinese Air Force was under strength and badly equipped. Initially, the Russians helped support the Chinese in their war against Japan, but by 1941 Chennault had managed to purchase 100 Curtiss Tomahawks and attract over 100 pilots on fixed one-year contracts. Training in Burma at RAF facilities, three squadrons flew the distinctive shark-tooth marked planes, making their first attack on Japanese aircraft on 20 December 1941. Later they operated over Burma, claiming more bombers and fighter escorts. Renamed the 23rd Fighter Group of the USAAF, they destroyed 13 enemy aircraft over Kweilin, and more over Hengyang, mounting a series of joint operations with the RAF; during the defence of Rangoon they downed 291 Japanese aircraft. The P-40s were replaced by P-51 Mustangs and from their formation to the end of hostilities they claimed 621 enemy aircraft shot down, with 320 destroyed on the ground.

◀ *LEFT: The insignia for the volunteer group the Flying Tigers.*

see Chiang Kai-Shek p. 125

CHIANG KAI-SHEK (1887–1975)

Chiang had become a nationalist supporter in the early 1900s while at military college. The leader of the Nationalists, Sun Yat-sen, died in March 1925 and Chiang emerged as his successor. After defeating the Communists in battle, Chiang set up government in Nanjing and pushed through a series of reforms. The Japanese invasion (1937) forced Chiang to agree with Mao Zedong, the Communist leader, to combat the Japanese.

In 1941 Chiang's army received support from Joseph Stilwell, commander of the US forces in China, Burma and India. Stilwell and Chiang disagreed on many issues, the former considering Chiang to be an inept military leader. The arguments caused the recall of Stilwell in

October 1944, and by the time of the Japanese collapse the Communists had the military upper-hand.

No sooner had the war ended than the Communists sought to gain control of China, which they finally achieved after a ruinous civil war, in October 1949. Mao Zedong was pronounced leader of the new Peoples' Republic of China. Chiang and what remained of his army and loyal supporters established an opposing regime in Taiwan. Chiang died in April 1975.

■ see Chinese Take Foochow and Nanning p. 295

▲ *ABOVE: Chinese General Chiang Kai-shek.*

TITO, JOSIP (1892–1981)

Tito had been captured by the Russians while serving for Austria-Hungary in World War I. He became a Communist and fought during the Russian Revolution. Tito returned to Yugoslavia, but when the government outlawed Communism he was arrested. He served five years in prison and was released in 1933. He returned to Russia, then fought during the Spanish Civil War, but after the German invasion of

Yugoslavia he headed home to help set up partisan units to fight the Germans. Tito ably led the partisans in their bloody struggle and in November 1943 he established a government in Bosnia. So great a risk was Tito that Hitler ordered an assassination attempt in February 1944. A new Yugoslavian government was established under Ivan Subasic in May 1944; Tito served as War Minister, but continued to lead his partisans until they had liberated Belgrade (October 1944). Tito became the Premier of Yugoslavia in March 1945 and created a new Federal Republic. In 1948, after a series of unresolved disputes with Russia, he broke with his mentors forever and pursued his own policies for Yugoslavia. Tito became Life President in 1974 and died on 4 May 1981.

TITO'S PARTISANS (1941–45)

Following the German invasion of Yugoslavia, Croatia was made an independent state, the Italians occupied parts of Slovenia, Montenegro, Kosovo and areas along the Dalmatian Coast. Bulgaria annexed Macedonia and the majority of Serbia, and eastern Slovenia was annexed by Germany. Two resistance organizations emerged: the Communists under Tito and the Serb royalist Chetniks. To begin with, both Partisan groups resisted occupation and in January 1943 the Germans and the Italians attempted to wipe out Partisan activity in a major offensive. A good grasp of tactics and difficult terrain saved Tito's men, who were on the ascendancy in terms of support. The Germans continued to battle with Tito's partisans, who were by now well supplied with captured equipment and were receiving additional assistance from British aircraft, which flew in supplies and advisors. The Germans continued to try to wipe out Tito's men until 1944, when they began their retreat from the Balkans. Tito was able to take

Belgrade just hours before the Russian army arrived. His men participated in the capture of Zagreb on 9 May 1945. Although pro-Soviet, post-war Yugoslavia found itself in the British-dominated zone of Europe, along with Greece and Albania.

◪ see Germans Attempt to Snatch Tito p. 228

CHETNIKS BATTLE WITH TITO (2 NOVEMBER 1941)

By November 1941 it was apparent that the Chetniks and Tito's Communists would never see eye to eye, either on the way in which to deal with the occupying forces or on the future of Yugoslavia. A civil war broke out between the two groups. Mihailovic met with the Germans on 11 November, to begin his collaboration with them.

◪ see Tito's Partisans p. 127

BRITISH LAUNCH THEIR LARGEST AIR OPERATION (7 NOVEMBER 1941)

Under continual pressure to step up its air offensive against Germany, Bomber Command launched nearly 400 aircraft against Berlin, Cologne and Manheim. To date this was the heaviest RAF offensive of the war. The flight to Berlin of 1,700 km (1,056 miles) succeeded in catching the Germans unaware, but at least 37 aircraft were lost as a result of poor weather conditions. The British had been routinely bombing German targets with increasing effect, but had needed to split their assets to deal with Italian targets around the Mediterranean, including Brindisi and Naples, which were bombed in the middle of November. Their aim was the prevention of Italian and German reinforcements arriving in North Africa.

◪ see Bomber Command p. 96

'THE SEA SHALL NOT HAVE THEM' (1939–45)

The vital task of recovering downed aircraft crews from the oceans grew increasingly important throughout the war. Apart from the moral obligation to rescue the men there was also the practical issue of having to replace experienced crew. The RAF Marine Craft section originated during World War I when small craft and their crews were transferred from the Royal Naval Air Service. The RAF developed the service during the 1930s and by the outbreak of the war had a network of launches and flying boats capable of going out in all weathers to search for ditched crews. Although there are no precise figures related to the number of

▼ *BELOW: Survivors from the HMS Ark Royal.*

men saved by these launches, it has been estimated that at least 14,000 men owed their lives to the RAF alone. Similar services had been set up by Australia and were active in the Pacific. Indeed, wherever British aircraft were posted, an RAF Marine Craft section unit was sent to deal with air-sea rescue. Shortly after the war the service was incorporated fully into the RAF and ultimately the helicopter took over many of the duties, but RAF men had served in the Middle East, the Mediterranean and all around the coasts of Europe.

◆ see Thousand-Bomber Raid p. 165

▲ ABOVE: The HMS Ark Royal sinks beneath the waves.

SINKING OF THE HMS *ARK ROYAL* (14 NOVEMBER 1941)

At 02:15 on 14 November 1941, just off the coast of Gibraltar, the HMS *Ark Royal* fell victim to an Italian submarine attack. The majority of the crew was saved. The vessel had been a continual thorn in the German and Italian sides since the beginning of the war and both countries had claimed to have sunk the ship in the past. The aircraft carrier slipped beneath the waters at around 06:00.

see Japanese Capture Hong Kong p. 141

OPERATION CRUSADER (18–28 NOVEMBER 1941)

General Cunningham's 8th Army launched Operation Crusader in order to reinforce Tobruk and hopefully recapture Cyrenaica and Tripolatiania. After initial successes, both the Italians and the Germans began to put up a stiff fight. In a major attack towards Tobruk, one British armoured brigade lost 113 of its 141 tanks. The Tobruk garrison managed to break out and join the 8th Army on 28 November and by the beginning of December the British had achieved a strategic success in North Africa. On 2 December Rommel launched a final attack against Tobruk, but could make no headway. Within a week, the supply corridor to Tobruk had been re-established by the British.

AUCHINLECK, CLAUDE (1884–1981)

Auchinleck was a career officer, having achieved the rank of Major-General by 1938, after he had spent time serving in Egypt, Aden (Yemen), Mesopotamia and India. He commanded the Allied Expeditionary Forces sent to Norway in 1940, but by July 1941 had taken over command of Allied troops in the Middle East. In November of the same year he launched Operation Crusader against the Axis forces in North Africa. The campaign initially appeared successful, but the following May Rommel launched his own counteroffensive. Auchinleck was hopelessly outmanoeuvred and large numbers of Allied troops were lost. Auchinleck's troops had outnumbered Rommel's men, yet Tobruk had fallen, with the loss of 35,000 British and Commonwealth troops; the British task force had been reduced to just 100 machines. Churchill replaced Auchinleck on 8 August 1942. In June 1943 Auchinleck took command of British forces in India, was knighted and became a full Field-Marshall in June 1945. Mountbatten forced him to resign in August 1947 (he was accused of being pro-Pakistani at this crucial time), but he remained in the army until his retirement in 1968.

▸ *see* Renewed German Offensive and Gazala Line p. 148

ASSAULT ON MOSCOW (21 NOVEMBER 1941)

The Germans seized Rostov by a frontal attack. The occupation was completed by 21 November, by which time lead German units had reached Istra, 30 miles to the north-west of Moscow. The Donetz industrial and mineral areas were now under German control. In appalling weather, the German advance began to slow and the Russians planned a series of counteroffensives.

▸ *see* Germans Abandon the Attack on Moscow p. 133

◂ *LEFT: The road to Moscow.*

BURMA CAMPAIGN (DECEMBER 1941–AUGUST 1945)

One of the main reasons for the campaign in Burma was the need to maintain an overland supply route to China, which would occupy a large percentage of the Japanese army. In the early months, the war was a disaster for the British: they were outmanoeuvred, outfought and forced to retreat from Burma to the comparative safety of India. The battles fought during the campaign were prosecuted despite malaria, typhus and monsoons. The chief units during the war were from the Indian Army, but Ghurkas, East and West Africans, other local ethnic groups, Americans, Canadians and Chinese would all participate against the Japanese invaders. The principle struggle was to reopen the Burma Road and the tactics deployed included the airlifting of entire divisions that needed to be re-supplied from the air. Jungle airstrips needed to be cut and as the area was criss-crossed with rivers these, too, needed to be patrolled and denied to the enemy. Had the Japanese been able to penetrate into India, any hope of displacing them would have been lost and often against great odds, scratch Allied units fought desperate actions in extremely difficult conditions.

◆ *see* Japanese Take Rangoon p. 155

GERMANS ABANDON THEIR ATTACK ON MOSCOW (5 DECEMBER 1941)

Reserves amounting to over 100 divisions and supported by 1,500 tanks, launched a counteroffensive against the 67 German divisions menacing Moscow on 5 December. The Germans were taken by surprise and the Russians penetrated German lines to a depth of 18 km (11 miles). The Russians continued offensive actions throughout December, but no major territory was lost. For the first time German casualties were mounting.

◆ *see* Germans Capture Sevastopol p. 170

PEARL HARBOR (7 DECEMBER 1941)

On 27 March 1941, the Japanese spy Takeo Yoshikawa arrived in Hawaii to study the US naval fleet, which had its base at Pearl Harbor on the island. His information provided the intelligence the Japanese needed to launch the pre-emptive attack on the US base that resulted in America's entry to the war.

The attack took place on 7 December 1941 and took the US completely by surprise. The The Japanese deployed six aircraft carriers and over 400 aircraft in the attacks, which killed 2,400 US personnel and accounted for 18 US vessels either sunk or badly damaged. As it transpired, the primary target had been the US aircraft carriers, which were on manoeuvres at the time, and subsequently the US Navy would use these carriers and submarines to first stop and then reverse Japanese fortunes in the Pacific. The attack did, however, give the Japanese six months breathing space to launch other invasions unmolested. The Japanese were aware of the fact that the US fleet could not be permanently neutralized, yet they missed the opportunity to destroy the vast oil reserves held at Pearl Harbor, which would have taken months to replace and at the same time have prevented the US fleet from taking any offensive actions. However, the attack on Pearl Harbor was a serious blow to the US, not just practically, but also in terms of morale.

Some 22 Japanese ships took part in the Pearl Harbor operation, but by 1945 only one would still be afloat. In the longer-term, the attack was a turning point in the war, assuaging any doubts the US had about joining the conflict.

◊ *see* Allies Declare War on Japan p. 137

▶ *RIGHT: The US fleet is attacked at anchor at the Hawaiian base Pearl Harbor.*

JAPANESE FIGHTER BOMBERS (DECEMBER 1941)

For the Japanese, seeking to extend an empire which was 90 per cent water, the primary imperative was to have access to aircraft that could find and destroy enemy targets on land or at sea. They therefore developed a range of fighter bombers, most of which were capable of taking off from aircraft carriers or from land-based airstrips. The Japanese reasoned that these aircraft were the eyes, ears and the main offensive arm of the Imperial Japanese Navy. As a result of this

▼ BELOW: Japanese bombers.

need for versatility the Japanese tended to develop smaller aircraft which had the capabilities of both fighters and small bombers. Some were adapted primarily to deliver torpedoes, such as the Kate and the Jill. Others were designed to deliver a single bomb, in effect a dive bomber, such as the Val, Nell and Betty. One hundred and forty-five Kates were used in the attack on Pearl Harbor, operating as torpedo and level bombers. They were also responsible for the sinking of three American aircraft carriers within the first 12 months of the war. By 1944 the Kate was obsolete; however 1,149 were built between 1936 and 1943.

ALLIES DECLARE WAR ON JAPAN (8 DECEMBER 1941)

In the aftermath of the Japanese attack on the naval base at Pearl Harbor, the United States and Britain declared war on the empire of Japan. On the same day the Japanese invaded the Philippines, Malaya and Hong Kong. On 10 December Japanese units landed on Guam to begin occupation. The Japanese had also landed at Bataan without opposition and the American garrisons in Shanghai and Tientsin in China were captured.

see Germany and Italy Declare War on the US p. 139

JAPAN INVADES SIAM AND MALAYSIA (8 DECEMBER 1941)

At 04:15 on 8 December, Japanese bombers began attacks on Singapore. Fearful of a Japanese invasion, HMS *Prince of Wales* and HMS *Repulse* were sent to intercept the Japanese invasion fleet. The Japanese had already landed at Khota Bharu on the east coast of Malaya, near the Thai border, and at Singora in Thailand itself. At this point all the British could do was carry out a reconnaissance.

see Japanese Capture Hong Kong p. 141

FIRST JEWS GASSED (8 DECEMBER 1941)

The Nazi concentration camp at Chelmno, which dealt with Jews from the Lodz ghetto, was the first fully functional extermination camp. Using mobile gas vans it claimed its first victims on 8 December 1941. The Nazis had converted 20 vans so that carbon monoxide could be pumped into the back; each could hold between 25 and 60 people. It has been estimated that around 700,000 Jews were killed in these vans, but the system had been tested on mentally ill Polish children. The vans were manned by one of the four Einsatzgruppen that operated in the Soviet Union. The Polish city of Lodz had a Jewish population of 223,000 before the Germans arrived; by 1945 there were just 6,000 left in the ghetto.

◑ *see* Gassing Begins at Auschwitz p. 144

SINKING OF THE *PRINCE OF WALES* AND THE *REPULSE* (10 DECEMBER 1941)

After leaving Singapore to intercept a Japanese invasion fleet, at 14:00 on 9 December the two British vessels were spotted by a Japanese submarine. Fortunately the captain gave the wrong coordinates and Japanese torpedo-carrying aircraft could not find either vessel. The following day, however, the Japanese found their targets and the *Prince of Wales* and *Repulse* were sunk by torpedoes and bombs. The *Prince of Wales* had been part of the fleet that accounted for the *Bismark*. It had also been the venue for the meeting between Roosevelt and Churchill in August 1941. The *Repulse* was more venerable and had been completed in 1916. It, too, hunted for the *Bismark* after undergoing a major refit, completed in 1936.

JAPANESE LAND AT LUZON (10 DECEMBER 1941)

Bangkok, the Thai capital, fell on 9 December 1941 and the following day Japanese troops landed at Luzon in the Philippines. The Americans resisted vigorously but were hopelessly outnumbered and faced powerful Japanese air support, which claimed a US destroyer and two submarines. With Tarawa and Makin in the Gilbert Islands already in Japanese hands, the Americans found it difficult to respond to attacks on so many fronts.

see Japanese Capture Hong Kong p. 141

GERMANY AND ITALY DECLARE WAR ON THE US (11 DECEMBER 1941)

Hitler, in the Reichstag and Mussolini, speaking from the balcony of the Plazzo Venezia, declared war on the US on 11 December. The US reciprocated in kind. In the House of Commons Churchill noted 'In Hitler's launching of the Nazi campaign on Russia we can already see, after less than six months of fighting, that he has made one of the outstanding blunders of history.'

see Japanese Invade Mindanao and Wake Island p. 139

CONVOY HG76 (14 DECEMBER 1941)

HG76 is seen as the beginning of the military strategy that led to the decisive convoy battle of early 1943 and the defeat of the U-boats. HG76 sailed from Gibraltar expecting a difficult voyage. For the first time, the Royal Navy destroyed a wolf pack of U-boats. The new escort tactics and information from the cracked German naval code led to the sinking of four of the nine U-boats attacking the convoy outside Gibraltar.

see Wolf Packs p. 26

JAPANESE INVADE MINDANAO AND WAKE ISLAND (20 DECEMBER 1941)

The Japanese landed on Davao on the island of Mindanao on 20 December 1941. The following day some 43,000 Japanese troops arrived to the north of Manila in the Gulf of Lingayen. At 13:00 on 22 December further Japanese landings took place at Bauang, Aringay and Agoo. That night Japanese troops began landing on Wake Island. The struggle for the Philippines was reaching its climax.

■ *see* Wake Island p. 140

WAKE ISLAND (22 DECEMBER 1941)

Japanese bombing had commenced on 8 December and continued for two days. At 05:00 the Japanese invasion fleet arrived off Wake Island, a small, v-shaped rock, 4,000 km (2,500 miles) west of Pearl Harbor. The first defence battalion could only muster around 385 men, but in the event the Japanese were only able to land on the adjacent Wilkes Island. The sheer weight of numbers and dwindling defenders meant that the Japanese took just 45 minutes to overrun the garrison once they arrived there. The defence troops had held out for 15 days and a quarter of their number had been killed or wounded. They had sunk four Japanese ships, damaged eight others, shot down 21 aircraft, damaged 50 more and inflicted over 1,000 casualties on the Japanese invasion force. The defenders would spend three years in Japanese prisoner of war camps. Wake Island was liberated by US troops on 14 May 1944. The US commander, Major Devereux, was subsequently awarded the Navy Cross.

■ *see* Japanese Take Manila p. 144

▲ ABOVE: The US attacks Japanese forces at Wake Island.

JAPANESE CAPTURE HONG KONG (25 DECEMBER 1941)

Japanese troops began their attack on Hong Kong on 18 December
and within 24 hours they were able to occupy half of the area. By
25 December the British garrison had been under siege for seven days.
At 09:00 they proposed their surrender terms and that afternoon the
British commander gave the order to surrender. Many local Chinese
welcomed the Japanese troops and waved Japanese flags at the columns
of troops.

◪ see Japanese Take Manila p. 144

1942

1 Jan	The United Nations is formed
2 Jan	The Japanese capture Manila
16 Jan	The Japanese attack Burma
20 Jan	The Wannsee Conference sets the Final Solution in motion
15 Feb	Singapore falls to the Japanese
27 Feb	The Battle of the Java Sea begins
5 Mar	General Alexander takes over as commander in Burma
7 Mar	Java falls to the Japanese
8 Mar	The Japanese take Rangoon
28 Mar	Allied forces attack St Nazaire
9 Apr	The Japanese capture Bataan
12 Apr	Mountbatten becomes Chief of Combined Operations
16 Apr	The citizens of Malta are awarded the Victoria Cross
18 Apr	The Dolittle air raid against Tokyo is launched
4 May	The Battle of the Coral Sea begins
5 May	Operation Ironclad begins in Madagascar
27 May	Heydrich is assassinated
30 May	The thousand-bomber raid is launched
4 June	The Battle of Midway begins
1 July	The Germans capture Sevastopol
26 July	The RAF begins a series of raids on Hamburg
7 Aug	US marines land on Guadalcanal
19 Aug	The Allies raid Dieppe
28 Aug	The Germans cross the Volga
30 Aug	The First Battle of El Alamein begins
15 Sept	The Battle of Stalingrad begins
8 Nov	Operation Torch is initiated

GASSING BEGINS AT AUSCHWITZ (JANUARY 1942)

Although the exact date of the start of mass gassings at Auschwitz is unknown, it is certain that the two associated camps had carried out experimental gassing on Russian prisoners of war around September 1941 and it is likely that the system started at Auschwitz itself in January 1942. Systems were set up effectively to deal with 6,000 people per day. Transports would regularly arrive from Poland, Slovakia, the Netherlands, Belgium and Yugoslavia. By January 1943 the first transports were arriving from Berlin itself and by May 1944 Hungarian Jews were beginning to arrive. In addition to the Jews murdered in the two camps, at least 20,000 gypsies were also liquidated and their bodies burned. Auschwitz became the largest graveyard in Europe, where almost a quarter of all murdered met their end.

see Heydrich is Attacked in Prague p. 163

CREATION OF THE UNITED NATIONS (1 JANUARY 1942)

By 1 January 1942, 26 nations – including the US, Great Britain, Russia, China, Greece, Norway and Yugoslavia – had signed the Atlantic Charter. In effect this was the creation of the United Nations. They were to 'Ensure life, liberty, independence and religious freedom and to preserve the rights of man and justice.' The 26 were implacably opposed to the Axis doctrine and purposes.

see Stalin and Churchill Meet in Moscow p. 176

JAPANESE TAKE MANILA (2 JANUARY 1942)

US and Filipino forces evacuated the area north of Manila on 2 January 1942, allowing the Japanese to consolidate their control of the Philippine capital. The US troops retreated towards the Bataan peninsula under constant attack, including air raids on the island of Corregidor. By

7 January the Japanese had forced all remaining US and Filipino units into the Bataan peninsula; they then proceeded towards the coast.

ZERO (1939–45)

The Zero (A6M) was undoubtedly the most famous of the Japanese aircraft of the war. It was nicknamed 'Zeke' by the Allies and was equally at home on an aircraft carrier or on land-based airfields. The first aircraft, designed and built by Mitsubishi, flew on 1 April 1939, the first of 11,000 aircraft. It was a small, fast and highly manoeuvrable aircraft with a maximum speed of around 500 kph

(311 mph). In the early years of the war, it out-performed anything used by the British and later the US, but by the Battle of Midway, the US Hellcats and Corsairs were more than a match for the Zero. For the Japanese, it was never a question of not having enough Zeros, it was finding the pilots that was problematic. As pilot losses mounted and US aircraft became more deadly, the Zero was no longer the force it had once been. Attempts were made to improve the performance, but after 1943 it could no longer compete. A newer version in 1945 came close, but by this stage it was too late to deal with the hundreds of US aircraft dominating the skies.

JAPANESE CAPTURE KUALA LUMPUR (10 JANUARY 1942)

The Indian 3rd Corps attempted to hold a line against the Japanese
between 8 and 9 January 1942 but the following day the British ordered
the abandonment of Kuala Lumpur, which was immediately occupied
by the Japanese. The Indian corps continued its retreat southward,
under heavy Japanese air attack. On 13 January additional British
reinforcements arrived in Singapore and were deployed across the
Malayan peninsular to hold off the Japanese attacks.

◆ see Japan Invades Siam and Malaysia p. 137

OPERATION PAUKENSCHLAG (11 JANUARY 1942)

Operation Paukenschlag ('Drumbeat') was a German campaign carried
out along the east coast of the United States. U-boats had been
intercepting British convoys around Newfoundland and it was now
proposed to attack the US coastline from New York to Florida. Five
U-boats began their attacks on 11 January, claiming their first victim
the following day. The operation ended on 6 February, having claimed
25 merchant ships and 156,939 tons of war materials.

◆ see Wolf Packs p. 26

JAPANESE INVADE BURMA (16 JANUARY 1942)

Japanese forces began
their offensive in Burma
by attacking Myitta and
Tavoy on 16 January.
Within three days

◀ LEFT: Japanese enter Rangoon.

Japanese troops were attacking in the Moulmein area and by 23 January they had achieved air superiority and were threatening Rangoon. There was a lull towards the end of the month as they began reorganizing for a new push. On 30 January the Japanese captured the airport at Moulmein and the following day began to shell Martaban.

◆ see Burma Campaign p. 133

SLIM, WILLIAM (1897–1970)

British commander William Slim served in Mesopotamia and at Gallipoli, where he was badly wounded and invalided out of the army during World War I. He persuaded the army to take him back and fought on the Western Front and then won a Military Cross during the capture of Baghdad. After a term serving in India he taught at the Camberley Staff College until 1937 and was then reposted back to India.

During World War II he fought in the Sudan, Abyssinia and Eritrea then in the Middle East until he was transferred to Burma in March 1942. Slim's summer 1943 offensive to capture Akyab ended in failure and he was ultimately succeeded by Mountbatten. In March 1944 he successfully defended Assam from the Japanese and participated in the offensive later that year, taking Mandalay in March 1945. His defence led to the British capture of Rangoon in May 1945.

After the war Slim became the Head of the Imperial Defence College, and in 1948 he succeeded Montgomery as Chief of the Imperial Staff. After retiring from the army he wrote his memoirs, served as the Governor of Australia and was made a peer in 1960. He died in December 1970.

◆ see Burma Campaign p. 133

WANNSEE CONFERENCE (20 JANUARY 1942)

This meeting at an SS-owned villa on the shore of a Berlin lake aimed to deal with the bureaucratic coordination to systematically slaughter 11 million Jews in Europe. This would be the vehicle by which the Final Solution would be handled. The essential points were to expel Jews from every sphere of life and from territories controlled by the Germans – effectively to 'cleanse' Europe of Jews. The conference not only identified the exact numbers and locations of all Jews in German territory, but also laid down the treatment and definition of a Jew as far as the Final Solution was concerned. Those who matched certain criteria with regard to mixed blood would be sterilized, all others would be eliminated. Some 537,000 Jews had already left German-controlled Europe by the end of October 1941. Since that date all emigration had been prohibited. Already hundreds of thousands, primarily those in Russia, had been killed and ultimately the Nazis would succeed in slaughtering between five and six million European Jews. Heydrich and Himmler would assume the leadership of the Final Solution.

■ see Goering Presents the Final Solution p. 116

RENEWED GERMAN OFFENSIVE AND GAZALA LINE (21 JANUARY–1 JULY 1942)

Rommel launched a major offensive towards Agedabia on 21 January 1942. The Axis troops advanced eastward, managing to outflank the prepared British defences. The British began to retire and by 25 January were on the road to Benghazi. By 1 July the British had been rolled all the way back into Egypt. This would be the high watermark of German successes in North Africa; soon it would be Rommel being chased across North Africa.

■ see Erwin Rommel p. 149

JAPANESE LAND IN THE SOLOMONS (23 JANUARY 1942)

Japanese troops began landing on New Guinea and Bougainville in the Solomon Islands on 23 January; they met very little opposition. In New Guinea Allied troops evacuated the capital, Lae, and Salamaua on 24 January, just a day before the Japanese landed. By 28 January they had taken Rossel Island, east of New Guinea, and were dangerously close to Australia. On 2 February the Japanese began to menace Port Moresby, the capital of Papua.

◆ see Japanese Capture Borneo Oilfields p. 150

ROMMEL, ERWIN (1891–1944)

Rommel, a career soldier, joined the German army in 1910, receiving the Iron Cross for bravery during World War I and remaining in the small interwar German army. In 1939 he was promoted to Major-General and served in Poland. Commanding 7th Panzer Division from February 1940, he planned the campaign against the western nations, launching the invasion and reaching Cherbourg on 19 June 1940.

In February 1941, he commanded the Deutsches Afrika Korps in Tripoli and swept across North Africa on the offensive. Despite setbacks he was only 240 km (150 miles) from Cairo

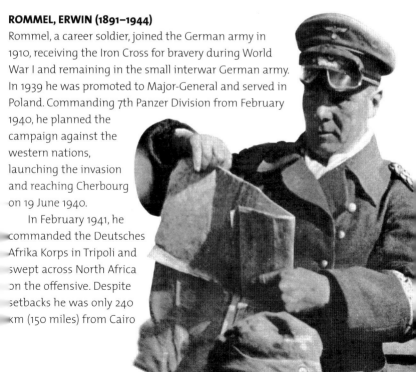

by the end of June 1942. At El Alamein he could make no further headway. The Allies launched their offensive in October, and pursued the 'Desert Fox' back across North Africa. He relinquished command in March, two months before the German surrender in North Africa.

Transferred to France in December 1943, to assist in the defence of Europe, Rommel was injured in an aircraft attack on 17 July 1944. Three days later – implicated in the plot to assassinate Hitler – he was given the choice of suicide or execution as a traitor; he chose suicide. Rommel was undoubtedly the most feared and respected of all German commanders.

◆ see Rommel Captures Tobruk and Enters Egypt p. 169

JAPANESE CAPTURE BORNEO OILFIELDS (6 FEBRUARY 1942)

The Japanese took Samarinda, off the east coast of Borneo on 6 February, and by 10 February their occupation of Borneo and Celebes was well underway. On 13 February they occupied Banjermasin and on the following day Japanese paratroops landed in Sumatra, forcing the Dutch garrison to retire. On 15 February the Japanese invasion fleet arrived off Sumatra and Allied troops headed for Java. Within four days the Japanese had invaded Bali.

◆ see Fall of Singapore p. 150

FALL OF SINGAPORE (15 FEBRUARY 1942)

Despite General Percival's defiance that Singapore would not fall while an Allied soldier still stood, on 8 February at 08:45, two Japanese divisions landed on the north-west coast. They were able to establish a bridgehead and Percival sent reinforcements the following day, but 15,000 Japanese troops managed to cross the waters between the Malayan mainland and the island of Singapore. In response the British withdrew from the west of the island and on 10 February they established a defence line. The subsequent counterattack was a failure. On 11 February General Yamashita ordered that leaflets be dropped on Singapore, asking the island to surrender. When this demand was ignored Japanese troops attacked along the whole of the Allied perimeter, forcing all Allied shipping to evacuate the harbour. The Japanese continued their attacks and with ammunition, food and water running out, Percival signed an unconditional surrender at 19:50 on 15 February. The Gibraltar of the east had fallen.

YAMASHITA, TOMOYUKI (1888–1946)

After serving as the Japanese military attaché in Germany between 1919 and 1922, Yamashita was posted to the Military Affairs Bureau and later took command of a brigade in Korea. Tojo sent him to Germany to investigate advancements in military technology and tactics and he advised the Japanese government to modernize before going to war.

Yamashita outmanoeuvred the British in Malaya and Singapore in 1942; he was promoted to a General in February 1943 and placed in command of the Philippines. When US forces under Douglas MacArthur landed at Mindoro (some 240 km/150 miles from Yamashita's headquarters at Manila), he moved his command to Luzon.

US troops ultimately landed at Luzon and Yamashita released his Allied prisoners of war and headed inland with his command. He attempted to form independent guerrilla units to resist the US invasion, but by this stage the war was coming to a close in the Pacific.

Yamashita was captured by US troops on 2 September 1945. He was held responsible for alleged Japanese atrocities on the Philippines during the war. Despite the sketchy evidence against him, he was found guilty and hanged on 23 February 1946.

see Battle of the Java Sea p. 153

MACARTHUR IS ORDERED TO LEAVE BATAAN (22 FEBRUARY 1942)

Under strict orders from President Roosevelt himself, General MacArthur left the Philippines on 22 February 1942, uttering promises to return. MacArthur transferred his headquarters to Australia. On 26 February a large Japanese amphibious invasion fleet left Luzon for Mindoro; if it fell, US troops based in Bataan would be completely cut off. On 1 March an advanced party of Japanese landed at Zamboango on Mindanao.

⬤ *see* Douglas MacArthur p. 152

MACARTHUR, DOUGLAS (1880–1964)

Douglas MacArthur was an outstanding West Point graduate, becoming the US army's youngest General in 1923. When the Japanese invaded the Philippines in 1941, MacArthur was decisively defeated, but pledged to return.

He was appointed Supreme Commander of the Southwest Pacific Area and, with Admiral Nimitz, planned a counteroffensive which led to the Battles of Midway and the Coral Sea. MacArthur advocated an island-hopping strategy by landing amphibious troops on key islands, whilst Nimitz blockaded larger Japanese garrisons on less important islands.

By early 1944 some 100,000 Japanese had been isolated and MacArthur now planned to retake the

Philippines. The battle of Leyte Gulf crippled the Japanese and on 9 January 1945 MacArthur landed, taking Manila in March. MacArthur's last major operation was against Okinawa (April 1945). It was a pyrrhic victory, but events were fast overtaking the general. Two atomic weapons were dropped on Japan in August and the Japanese surrendered.

In 1950 MacArthur took command of UN forces in Korea, but was removed the following year after requesting the use of nuclear weapons against North Korea and China. He died in April 1964.

BATTLE OF THE JAVA SEA (27 FEBRUARY–1 MARCH 1942)
In an attempt to prevent the invasion of Java, an Allied task force intercepted the Japanese near Surabaya. The squadron of five cruisers and 11 destroyers suffered heavy casualties: three were sunk, two were badly damaged and the rest were incapable of further offensive actions. They landed the following day, encountering little opposition. By 3 March Japanese forces were close enough to Australia to begin air raids.

see Japanese Capture Java p. 155

ALEXANDER IS APPOINTED COMMANDER IN BURMA (5 MARCH 1942)
In early March, General Alexander replaced General Wavell as commander of Allied forces in Burma. Wavell had already given orders that Allied troops would withdraw from Rangoon and Alexander immediately ordered counterattacks in order to relieve Pegu and to close the gap between the 17th Indian Division and the 1st Burmese Division. Rangoon was evacuated on 7 March and the Japanese 33rd Division marched into the city.

see Harold Alexander p. 154

◄ LEFT: US commander General Douglas MacArthur.

ALEXANDER, HAROLD (1891–1969)

Harold Alexander was a Sandhurst graduate and during World War I fought with the Irish Guards, obtaining the rank of Brigadier. He fought in the Baltic Landwehr against the Communists in Latvia in 1919. He returned to more conventional duties, serving time in India and being promoted to the rank of Major General in 1937. He was given command of the 1st division of the British Expeditionary Force when they went to France in 1939. It was Alexander's men who covered the retreat and evacuation at Dunkirk. Alexander was then sent to Burma, but he was unable to stop the Japanese and after a short time he took command in Egypt and worked closely with Montgomery in forging the victory in North Africa. It was Alexander who organized the attacks on the Gustav Line and Monte Cassino in particular. After the war Alexander became the Governor General of Canada until 1952 and then served as Minister of Defence under Winston Churchill. He resigned from office in 1954 and concentrated on writing his autobiography, published in 1961. He died on 16 June 1969.

◆ see Burma Campaign p. 133

▲ ABOVE: British commander Harold Alexander.

JAPANESE CAPTURE JAVA (7 MARCH 1942)

By 1 March 1942, with the Allied fleet badly mauled and Allied aircraft destroyed, the Japanese spread out across Java, while Allied ships headed for Australia. On 2 March the Japanese captured the capital, Batavia, and the Dutch were forced to fall back, destroying everything that they left behind them. Finally, on 7 March, Java fell to the Japanese. The Dutch government had fled to Australia and what remained of the garrisons surrendered to the Japanese.

◆ *see* Japanese Capture Bataan p. 157

JAPANESE TAKE RANGOON (8 MARCH 1942)

On 5 March 1942 Alexander arrived in Rangoon and took command of all troops in Burma. He ordered an immediate counteroffensive but the Japanese had already attacked Pegu and cut off the road to Rangoon. Alexander, now aware of the severity of the situation, ordered Rangoon to be evacuated. The garrison at Pegu was ordered to break out and head north and on 8 March the Japanese entered Rangoon, with Indian infantry managing to break through the Japanese lines in order to allow the Allied troops to retire. The retreat continued and new Allied headquarters were set up near Mandalay.

◆ *see* The Chindits p. 189

RAID ON ST NAZAIRE (28 MARCH 1942)

At 01:34 on 28 March 1942, Operation Chariot literally hit home against St Nazaire at the mouth of the Loire River, when HMS *Campbeltown* rammed the dock gates. The port was a vital dry dock – indeed the only one available to the Germans on the Atlantic coast. It was capable of taking vessels as large as the *Tirpits*, but was primarily used as a U-boat base. The task force, consisting of a number of motor boats and torpedo boats, in addition to the converted destroyer, carried a compliment of 200 men from No. 2 Commando, along with demolition teams from eight other commando units. When the *Campbeltown* hit the dock gates at 20 knots, the Commandos fanned out across the harbour and placed charges to destroy German facilities. As they escaped in launches down river, five tons of explosives on board *Campbeltown* put the dry dock out of action for the remainder of the war. A German ship in the estuary tried to stop the Commandos and naval crew from escaping, but she was misidentified and sunk by German coastal batteries.

◆ *see* Commandos p. 156

COMMANDOS (1941–45)

Commandos were involved in the war for the first time in December 1941, at Vaagso in Norway, then in Dieppe in August 1942. On 6 June 1944 their objective, as part of the 1st Special Service Brigade, was the capture of the River Orne bridges, under the command of Lord Lovat. Operating with elements of 45 Commando, 6 Commando and the 6th Airborne Division, No. 3 Commando took the bridges and held them against German counterattacks. The Commandos are credited with 38 battle honours between 1940 and 1945 and were involved in raids and attacks at St Nazaire (28 March 1942), a fine early example of combined operations. The force consisted of 200 men from No. 2 Commando, who stormed ashore to destroy enemy installations. Churchill much favoured the existence of the Commandos.

◆ *see* Wolf Packs p. 26

AIR ASSAULT ON MALTA (2–8 APRIL 1942)

Although Malta had been under attack for nearly four months by April 1942, some of the most vicious raids took place in the first week of that month. On 5 April a British destroyer was sunk and two others were badly damaged in Valletta harbour; on 7 April the island suffered its heaviest attack, its 2,000th of the war. Control of Malta's harbour and airfields were imperative.

◆ *see* Malta VC p. 159

JAPANESE CAPTURE BATAAN (9 APRIL 1942)

On 8 April 1942 the American perimeter on the Bataan peninsular collapsed; 2,000 men managed to escape to Corregidor. At 12:30 on 9 April the unconditional surrender came into effect. During the capture the Japanese had netted 67,000 prisoners; thousands more would die during the Bataan death march that followed the capture of the city. Within hours of the surrender Corregidor came under artillery fire and the Japanese found themselves free to make an assault on the island of Cebu.

BATAAN DEATH MARCH (APRIL 1942)

On 9 April, after almost four months of resistance, the US and Filipino garrison of Bataan surrendered to the Japanese troops. The following day, the march north began towards Camp O'Donnell. Any man who faltered was summarily executed by the guards. Of the 9,300 US troops on the march, up to 650 died en route; casualties amongst the Filipinos were higher – of the 45,000 at least 5,000 died. The casualties at Camp O'Donnell were no better: in the first 40 days, some 1,500 US troops died and by the end of July the Filipino death toll had broken 20,000. This forced the Japanese to move the prisoners to a new camp at Cabanatuan, where they were joined by more US prisoners taken at Corregidor.

◆ *see* Battle of the Coral Sea p. 162

MOUNTBATTEN IS APPOINTED CHIEF OF COMBINED OPERATIONS (12 APRIL 1942)

Mountbatten managed to jump several ranks when he was named Chief of Combined Operations; with it he claimed a seat on the Chiefs of Staff Committee. He was given senior ranks in the army, navy and air force in order to validate his position. He would oversee a number of commando operations, including Dieppe and St Nazaire. This was a post he would hold until early 1943.

◘ *see* Louis Mountbatten p. 158

MOUNTBATTEN, LOUIS (1900–79)

Lord Louis Mountbatten was the great-grandson of Queen Victoria. He initially became a career naval officer, seeing action during the Norway campaign and serving as captain of the HMS *Kelly*, which was sunk off Crete in May 1940. His father had been born in Austria and because of anti-German sentiment in Britain the family had changed their name from Battenberg to Mountbatten.

On 21 October 1941 Mountbatten was appointed Head of Combined Operations command; he organized a number of commando raids, notably the Dieppe Raid in August 1942. Churchill had elevated Mountbatten to the simultaneous ranks of Vice-Admiral, Lieutenant-General and Air Marshal, much against the wishes of the military establishment. In October 1943 Mountbatten assumed command of South-East Asia Command (SEAC), charged with dealing with the Japanese in Singapore and Burma.

After the war Mountbatten, as Viceroy of India, steered India and Pakistan towards independence. He commanded the Mediterranean fleet between 1952 and 1955, followed by four years as First Sea Lord. He served as Chief of Defence staff from 1959 to 1965.

On 27 August 1979 Mountbatten was a victim of Irish terrorism when his boat was destroyed near one of his homes in County Sligo.

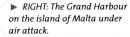 *see* Dieppe Raid p. 177

MALTA VC (16 APRIL 1942)

On 16 April 1942, after suffering some four months of daily attacks, King George VI awarded the George Cross, the civilian Victoria Cross, to the island of Malta. The King praised the heroism and devotion of its people. Malta represented a constant thorn in Rommel's side and since assuming command in North Africa he had made it a priority to subdue the island. Up until this point very little in the way of supplies had managed to get through to Malta and the island was under continual threat from up to 600 German and Italian aircraft based in Sicily. A handful of Spitfires remained in operation throughout the aerial siege and bombardment. The first Allied convoy made it safely into Malta on 14 August 1942.

see Convoy HG76 p. 139

▶ RIGHT: *The Grand Harbour on the island of Malta under air attack.*

▲ ABOVE: James Doolittle, with the airmen who took part in the raids on Tokyo.

DOOLITTLE RAID (18 APRIL 1942)

After Pearl Harbor, there was an outcry for revenge against the Japanese. On 18 April 1942 twenty-four crews were selected from the 17th Bombardment Group. The planes took off from the ocean off the Japanese coast, led by Lieutenant Colonel James H. Doolittle. They launched from USS *Hornet* in modified B-25s – destination Tokyo. They achieved complete surprise when they dropped the first bombs on the Japanese city. All but one of the aircraft made it to their landing spot in China. Doolittle himself bailed out just north of Chuchow and linked up with Chinese guerrillas. He was promoted to Brigadier General and awarded the Medal of Honor. In terms of damage, the raid had been a failure but the purpose was to prove to the American public and the Japanese authorities that Japan was not impervious to attack.

B-25 (1942)

The North American B-25 Mitchell medium bomber was undoubtedly one of the most famous US aircraft of World War II. It was the aircraft chosen by Doolittle when he raided Tokyo in April 1942; it would see service in virtually every region of combat and in addition to US use it would also be flown by British, Dutch, Australian and Russian pilots. It was primarily designed as a medium-altitude bomber, but it was used extensively against Japanese airfields at low level or for strafing or bombing attacks on Japanese shipping. Nearly 10,000 B-25s were built during the war. The aircraft had a maximum speed of 443 kph (275 mph), a range of 1,930 km (1,200 miles) and a service ceiling of 7,620 m (25,000 ft). The B-25 was affectionately known as the 'Heavenly Body'.

◐ see B-29s Carry Out First Raid on Japan p. 236

▼ BELOW: The B-25 bomber.

BATTLE OF THE CORAL SEA (4–8 MAY 1942)

This was the first major aircraft-carrier engagement of the war. In April 1942, Japanese forces left Rabaul to launch amphibious attacks on Port Moresby and Tulagi in the Solomon Islands. Three Japanese fleets set sail, but the US was alerted by intercepts.

The Japanese successfully took Tulagi on 3 May, but the following day the USS *Yorktown* launched three air strikes, then sailed south to rendezvous with the *Lexington*. A second Japanese fleet headed for the Solomons and was attacked by B-17s on 6 May. Unfortunately the two fleets failed to find each other and on 8 May Japanese aircraft hit the two US carriers; *Lexington* was abandoned and scuttled, but the Japanese carrier *Shokaku* was also crippled.

Meanwhile, the Allied surface fleet had come within range of the land-based Japanese aircraft on Rabaul and were attacked throughout the day. They were all that stood between the Japanese and Port Moresby. The Japanese panicked at the size of the US fleet and recalled their own. The *Yorktown* proceeded to Pearl Harbor, the *Shokaku* was out of action and the *Zuikaku* lacked aircraft.

▼ *BELOW: The US aircraft carrier* Lexington *explodes.*

JAPANESE PACIFIC FLEET

When Japan entered the war its Pacific fleet consisted of 10 battleships, 11 aircraft carriers, 18 heavy cruisers, 23 light cruisers, 129 destroyers, 67 gun boats and an assortment of auxiliary craft. When it faced British opposition, it had a distinct advantage in terms of its carrier-strike capacity. To support the fleet there were 1,540 aircraft, including the Zero – perhaps the best aircraft in the skies at the time. As it transpired, many of the Japanese ships were superior in design and in their weight-to-firepower ratios. Their crews had been well trained and extremely determined against massive odds.

see Battle of Midway p. 167

OPERATION IRONCLAD (5 MAY 1942)

The British Force 121 landed unopposed near the main town of Diego Suarez on 5 May 1942, in the first stage of the operation known as Ironclad. The Vichy French-held island of Madagascar initially resisted, but it was soon overcome. The Vichy retreated into the interior and continued to oppose the invasion and did not surrender until 6 November. Some 8,000 men were captured, along with vessels and aircraft.

see Pétain and Vichy France p. 47

HEYDRICH IS ATTACKED IN PRAGUE (27 MAY 1942)

Two Czech agents working for the British were parachuted close to Prague in an assassination attempt on Reinhard Heydrich. They awaited him on a street corner, knowing his car would be forced to slow down. When the moment came, however, their machine guns jammed and instead they threw a grenade into the car. Despite being wounded, Heydrich returned fire with his pistol and then collapsed. He died of blood poisoning on 4 June, caused by horse hair in the upholstery.

see Reinhard Heydrich p. 164

▲ ABOVE: Reinhard Heydrich.

HEYDRICH, REINHARD (1902–42)

Heydrich joined the Freikorps and then the German navy, where he was made Second Lieutenant in 1926. Forced to resign his commission in 1931, he joined the Nazi Party, becoming a member of the Schutzstaffel (SS) and later the Sicherheitsdienst (SD) – the SS security and intelligence service. He became Brigadier-General in 1933.

Together with Himmler, Heydrich was responsible for rounding up Hitler's opponents from January 1933; many were sent to Dachau. Heydrich became second in command (under Himmler) of the Gestapo, purging the Nazi Party; by 1935 the SD and Gestapo were accountable only to Hitler.

Heydrich forged documents implicating Russian generals in a plot against Stalin in 1937, while undermining his German political opponents. After the fall of Poland (1939), Heydrich formed death squads to liquidate leading Polish figures, followed by the two million Jews in Poland. Heydrich's SS Einsatz began a slaughter in the east as German influence grew.

Heydrich convened the Warsaw Conference in Berlin in January 1942 to coordinate the extermination of the European Jewish population, but was attacked by Czechoslovakian agents in Prague, dying from blood poisoning a few days later. On Hitler's orders, the Czech village of Lidice was liquidated in reprisal.

see Lidice Reprisals p. 168

▼ *BELOW: Waves of bombers launch a raid over Germany.*

THOUSAND-BOMBER RAID (30 MAY 1942)

The first RAF thousand-bomber raid (actually employing 1,047 bombers) struck Cologne on 30 May 1942. They had reached their target by midnight, where the aircraft dropped 2,000 tons of bombs on the city, reducing 13,000 houses to rubble and damaging 6,000 more. Civilian casualties were put at 469, with 4,500 wounded. The British lost around 40 bombers and 45 others were badly damaged. Of the raid Goering wrote 'Of course, the effects of aerial warfare are terrible if one looks at individual cases. But we have to accept them.' Even at this early stage it appears that Goering had accepted that Allied aircraft would be able to hit targets at will due to the impotence of his Luftwaffe.

ROYAL AIR FORCE RAIDS THE RUHR (1 JUNE 1942)

Hard on the heels of the thousand-bomber raid on Cologne, the RAF switched targets to hit the Ruhr area and Essen – both major German industrial targets. This time the RAF mustered 1,036 bombers. Around 31 RAF aircraft were lost; this was an integral part of Bomber Harris's blanket bombing strategy, aimed at disrupting and ultimately destroying German morale and economy. The scale of the two attacks were four times larger than the worst raid London had so far suffered. At this point the RAF was using a mixture of bombers, including the Wellington, the Halifax, the Sterling and the Lancaster.

LANCASTER BOMBER (1941–45)

The Lancaster, designed by Roy Chawick, made its maiden flight in January 1941. It was not an easy aircraft to construct as it consisted of 55,000 separate parts, it was therefore unsurprising that peak production only reached 293, in August 1944. Lancasters flew their first operational flight in March 1942; they would account for 64 per cent of all of the bomb tonnage dropped by the RAF during the war and would be immortalized as the aircraft that delivered the attacks during the Dambuster's raid and the sinking of the *Tirpits*. Some 7,377 Lancasters were built, of which 3,932 were lost. In total, Lancasters flew 156,000 sorties and dropped 608,612 tons of bombs. Bomber Harris himself said of the Lancaster: 'The finest bomber of the war! Its efficiency was almost incredible, both in performance and in the way it could be saddled with ever-increasing loads without breaking the camel's back. The Lancaster won the naval war by destroying over one-third of the German submarines in their ports.... The Lancaster won the air war by taking the major part in forcing Germany to concentrate on building and using fighters to defend the Fatherland.'

◆ *see* USAAF Arrives in Britain p. 170

BATTLE OF MIDWAY (4–7 JUNE 1942)

This engagement took place a month after the Battle of the Coral Sea and is considered by many to be the classic example of aircraft-carrier warfare. The Japanese hoped to destroy the US carrier fleet and thereby open up Hawaii to invasion. At dawn on 4 June, Japanese aircraft bombed Midway base. The US had broken the Japanese cipher codes, however, and Spruance, the commander of the US carrier group knew that if he hit the Japanese now they would be helpless as they attempted to refit and refuel their aircraft.

Spruance's attack, although costly, left three Japanese carriers ablaze. Japanese aircraft then crippled the USS *Yorktown*. A retaliatory strike from the USS *Enterprise* accounted for the final Japanese aircraft carrier, the *Hiryu*, along with the cruisers *Mogami* and *Mikuma*.

Spruance had won a decisive victory and promptly retired before Japanese submarines and surface vessels could find his carriers. The Japanese offensive ability had been destroyed; from this point Japan would be on the defensive. It had been just six months since the very same aircraft carriers had launched their aircraft against Pearl Harbor.

see Pearl Harbor p. 134

◄ *LEFT: Survivors of the USS* Yorktown.

US PACIFIC FLEET (1941–45)

In assessing the relative strengths of the US and Japanese fleets on the eve of the US entry into the war, it is perhaps more useful to consider the combined Allied fleets despite the fact that they did not always operate under the same command. It should also be appreciated that at least half the available US vessels were actually engaged in the Atlantic and not the Pacific. Taking this into account it leaves the combined Allied fleet in the Pacific at 10 battleships, nine of which were American; one British battle cruiser; three American aircraft carriers; 14 heavy cruisers, of which one was American; 22 light cruisers, 11 of which were American, seven British, three Dutch and one French; 100 destroyers, of which 80 were American, 13 British and seven Dutch; and 69 submarines, 56 of which were American and 13 Dutch. The comparative balance in aircraft was considerably in the Japanese favour – the Allies could only muster 650. In terms of the overall strength and effectiveness of the American Pacific fleet in particular, it was extremely providential that their aircraft carriers escaped the attack at Pearl Harbor.

see Japanese High Watermark p. 173

LIDICE REPRISALS (10 JUNE 1942)

German reprisals following the assassination of Heydrich were brutal. Three thousand Czechs were arrested; 2,000 were shot or died during interrogations. Czech police, under German orders, surrounded the village of Lidice (10 km/6 miles from Prague) rounding up the population. Killings began at 05:00 on 10 June 1942; all men and boys were shot and the remaining civilians taken to concentration camps. Of the 300, 143 survived. The village was burned to the ground.

see Jews Deported from Warsaw p. 172

ROMMEL CAPTURES TOBRUK AND ENTERS EGYPT (24 JUNE 1942)

By 12 June 1942 Rommel was within 24 km (15 miles) of Tobruk and British troops were retiring towards the Egyptian frontier. Churchill was alarmed and telegraphed Auchinleck, saying 'Presume there is no question in any case of giving up Tobruk'. There was certainly no intention, but by 14 June Rommel's troops had reached the Tobruk perimeter. Within three days Tobruk was cut off and the bulk of the British army had retreated beyond Bardia by 19 June. On 21 June Klopper, the commander of Tobruk, requested authority to surrender and terms were discussed. Thirty-thousand men, 2,000 tons of petrol, 5,000 tons of food and 2,000 vehicles fell into Rommel's hands; 70 per cent of the Afrika Korps were dead.

◀ *see* First Battle of El Alamein p. 179

▼ BELOW: Rommel's troops overcoming British traps in Tobruk.

GERMANS CAPTURE SEVASTOPOL (1 JULY 42)

Sevastopol had been cut off for months, its 100,000-strong garrison situated behind a triple defence line of trenches, minefields and forts. After suffering 46,000 shells and 20,000 tons of bombs, the defences began to crack and one by one the major forts were taken by German and Romanian troops. Finally, on 1 July, the defences were overrun and Sevastopol fell into German hands.

◆ see Germans Drive for the Caucasus p. 172

USAAF ARRIVES IN BRITAIN (1 JULY 1942)

The lead elements of the 8th Army Air Force, flying B-17s, arrived in Prestwick in Britain on 1 July 1942. The 8th would fly B-17 Flying Fortresses and B-24 Liberators in daylight bombing operations against Germany. Unlike Bomber Command, it was intended that they would make precision bombing runs; however, many of the results were indiscriminate and often equal damage was done to civilian targets.

◆ see Flying Fortress p. 170

FLYING FORTRESS (1941–45)

The first B-17 had its maiden flight on 28 July 1935, but by the time the US entered the war in December 1941 only a handful of the aircraft were in operation. The B-17 would be used primarily for daylight strategic bombing of enemy targets and by the time production ended in May 1945 some 12,726 of the aircraft had been built. The B-17 received its name the 'Flying Fortress' because of its awesome destructive fire power. In tight box formations it was perfectly capable of looking after itself with 13 machine guns bristling from its superstructure. B-17s flying out of Britain, mainly with the 8th Air Force, would endure an eight-hour return flight in order to bomb strategic targets in Germany.

Until the last few months of the war many of these aircraft flew with no fighter escort. It has been estimated that around 4,735 of them were lost in combat missions during the war. It is believed that less than 15 are still capable of flight today, as most were scrapped in the post-war years, or sold as surplus. In fact the jet aircraft was paramount in making the B-17 obsolete.

see Royal Air Force Raid Hamburg p. 174

▲ ABOVE: B-17 Flying Fortresses.

GERMANS DRIVE FOR THE CAUCASUS (9 JULY 1942)

In a change of strategy, the primary weight and thrust of the German assaults in Russia were diverted from the capture of Moscow to the overrunning of the Russian oil fields in the Caucasus. In the coming months this would have a massive impact on the outcome of the war. Army Group B was given the task of advancing on Stalingrad then along the River Volga towards Astrakhan.

⬘ *see* Germans Reach the Volga p. 179

JEWS DEPORTED FROM WARSAW (11 JULY 1942)

The Warsaw ghetto was created by the Germans in 1940 and served as a repository for Polish Jews before they were deported to one of the concentration or extermination camps – the first Jews departed the ghetto on 11 July 1942. It has been estimated that 370,000 Jews from the Warsaw ghetto were killed. The deportation reached a climax in 1943, when it was no longer practicable to carry out executions in Warsaw on a mass scale.

ZYKLON B (1942–45)

Zyklon B was the commercial name given to the poison hydrogen cyanide. It was chosen by the Germans to produce quicker and more effective results in the extermination chambers housed in the concentration camps. The pellets or discs were originally developed as a powerful insecticide, but it was discovered that when they interacted with iron or concrete, they would release hydrogen cyanide gas. The gas entered the blood and produced a form of internal asphyxiation as it blocked the oxygen released from red blood cells. Zyklon B had been developed in Germany by I. G. Farben and it was used initially to control lice in the concentration camps.

⬘ *see* Death Camps p. 174

▲ *ABOVE: Allied troops wait to catch Japanese snipers.*

JAPANESE HIGH WATERMARK (21 JULY 1942)

Around 21 July 1942, the maximum expansion and conquest of the Japanese was reached when they landed on Gona and Buna in New Guinea. The US Solomon Islands Invasion Fleet was already on its way from New Zealand to rendezvous near Fiji. By 26 July the expeditionary force had rendezvoused with other units and was proceeding towards the Solomon Islands and by the end of the month US bombers were pounding Guadalcanal.

◆ *see* US Marines Land at Guadalcanal p. 175

ROYAL AIR FORCE RAID HAMBURG (26–29 JULY 1942)

Harris and his Bomber Command, continuing the strategy of disrupting civilian and economic life in Germany, launched a series of raids, beginning on 26 July, on Hamburg, Danzig and other German targets. Harris promised to 'scourge the Third Reich from end to end'. In his broadcast in German, he told enemy civilians to expect air raids 'every night and every day, rain, blow or snow'.

⬙ see First USAAF Raid p. 176

▲ *ABOVE: Prisoners at Buchenwald.*

DEATH CAMPS (1942–45)

The term 'death camp' actually encompasses both the concentration camps and the extermination camps that collectively processed and held many millions of individuals during the war. The death camps were used to administer the German Final Solution and between 1941 and 1945 at least six million Jews alone were either slaughtered in or near their homes, by firing squads, murdered in mobile gas vans or in much larger numbers sent direct to extermination camps where they would be gassed. Many of the concentration camps, whilst ostensibly slave-labour facilities, simply meant a more lingering death from starvation and brutal treatment. The major concentration camps were Dachau, Sachsenhausen, Buchenwald, Mauthausen, Flossenburg, Ravensbruck, Auschwitz, Natzweiler, Neuengamme and Gross-rosen. Invariably the experience of both British, American and Russian troops who eventually liberated the camps was that the vast majority of the inmates had deteriorated physically to such an extent that they were virtually beyond help.

◆ see Extermination Camps Become Operational p. 87

US MARINES LAND AT GUADALCANAL (7 AUGUST 1943)

At 09:00 on 7 August 1942, 10 US marines began landing on Guadalcanal as part of the operations associated with the liberation of the Solomon Islands. They established a bridgehead and by nightfall they had penetrated a mile inland. Over the next few days waves of Japanese aircraft would attack fleets supporting the marines. By 8 August the marines had built an airstrip on Guadalcanal and by 19 August there were 11,000 US troops on the island. Throughout August and September the Japanese continued to reinforce and there was vicious fighting throughout September and October; neither side made headway. On 23 October the Japanese failed in a massive counterattack and a week

▶ RIGHT: US marines with a Japanese flag captured at Guadalcanal.

later the US Marines took the offensive and gained considerable ground. On 12 November a vicious sea battle took place, resulting in heavy casualties for both sides. Another US offensive in January finally paid off and by the following month they had control of the island. Japanese losses were estimated at 9,000; US losses were in excess of 2,000.

■ *see* Battle of the Bismarck Sea p. 192

STALIN AND CHURCHILL MEET IN MOSCOW (12 AUGUST 1942)

This was the first Moscow conference, attended by Stalin, Churchill and Averell Harriman (representing Roosevelt), as well as a representative for de Gaulle. The meeting continued until 15 August and discussed the possibility of opening a second front in Europe. Stalin demanded that pressure be taken off his armies; Churchill, not yet prepared, felt a demonstration would come in the form of the Dieppe raid.

■ *see* Casablanca Conference p. 186

FIRST USAAF RAID (17 AUGUST 1942)

Escorted by RAF Spitfires, 12 B-17 Flying Fortresses of the 8th US Army Air Force – which had arrived in Britain the previous month – launched their first major bombing attack on German-held Europe. The targets were the railway yards at Rouen in France. Between August 1942 and the end of the year, B-17s and B-24s (which began arriving in September) would make 1,547 flights, losing 32 aircraft.

LIBERATOR (1939–45)

Although some 19,256 B-24 Liberators were constructed, it is still a lesser-known aircraft than the B-17 Flying Fortress. It made its maiden flight on 28 December 1939 and initially the US military proposed its use as a high-altitude bomber. The aircraft would be deployed primarily in daytime bombing raids and initially they flew without fighter support. On 17 August 1943, 59 Liberators were shot down in one raid. Collectively Liberators dropped 630,000 tons of bombs during the war. B-24s would operate in all the major theatres throughout the remainder of the war and, in addition to their bombing duties, others would fly mine-laying missions, carry cargo and fuel and go on photographic reconnaissance missions. The B-24H/J, one of the most common variants, had a maximum speed of 467 kph (290 mph) and had a maximum range of 3,380 km (2,100 miles). It could operate at 8,534 m (28,000 ft). The aircraft could carry around six tons of bombs in each mission and it was particularly well suited for long range raids. The Liberator was variously known as Ford's Folly or the Flying Box Car. It is believed that no more than three B-24s still remain airworthy today.

◉ see USAAF Targets Germany p. 188

DIEPPE RAID (19 AUGUST 1942)

Under the direction of Lord Mountbatten, a major Allied raid was launched on Dieppe on 19 August 1942. The force of 5,000 Canadians, 1,000 British and elements of American Rangers and Free French arrived off the coast at 03:00. Things began to go seriously wrong when troops landed on the wrong beach and the invasion fleet ran into enemy vessels. The Canadians landed on the main beach and were pinned down instantly; their Churchill tanks were trapped. By 09:00 it was apparent that the raid had been a failure. Fifteen hundred prisoners were taken by the Germans, 28 tanks were lost, as well as several vessels and, in the skies above, the Allies lost 95 aircraft but shot down over 80 German aircraft and damaged a further 100 planes.

◉ see Louis Mountbatten p. 158

CHURCHILL TANK (1942–45)

The Churchill, designed to replace the Matilda, initially had a crew of seven, a speed of 24 kph (15 mph), a 2pdr and two machine guns. In March 1942 a major redesign led to the Mk III armed with a 6pdr. The next had a cast turret (Mk IV) and the Mk V an improved 6pdr. Churchill Mks I and II were used in Dieppe in August 1942, with deep-wading equipment. The Churchill proved its worth, particularly during the Italian campaign. The Mk VI began production in November 1943 with the 75-mm gun, in addition to a heavier version (Mark VII). Churchills were converted for a variety of specialized roles, notably the Assault Vehicle Royal Engineers (AVRE), which was armed with a 290-mm Petard mortar and designed for carpet-laying, bridge-laying and mine-clearing.

◻ see D-Day Beaches p. 232

GERMANS REACH THE VOLGA (28 AUGUST 1942)

In their push towards Stalingrad, advanced units of the German army reached the River Volga on 28 August, and had pushed forward to the western suburbs of the city by 3 September. The battle for Stalingrad began its first phase with massive German air assaults supporting the ground troops. Both sides poured in reinforcements and reserves, the weather deteriorated and by 13 September, after four weeks, the German 6th Army controlled the bulk of the city.

◆ *see* Battle of Stalingrad p. 180

FIRST BATTLE OF EL ALAMEIN (30 AUGUST 1942)

At 23:00 on 30 August Rommel launched an offensive along the whole of the El Alamein front. The battle became known as Alam el Halfa as it was

mainly concentrated around this ridge, which lay to the south-east of El Alamein. Rommel intended to turn the British positions and surround the 8th Army. By just the following day it was clear that he was failing. The RAF, the 7th Armoured Division, minefields and a shortage of fuel all proved insurmountable obstacles. On 1 September he tried again but was driven back, by which time the initiative had passed to the British, who were preparing to counterattack. By 2 September Rommel's troops had fallen back to their starting line to wait for a British counteroffensive that never materialized.

◀ *LEFT: Forces landing before the Battle of El Alamein.*

179

DESERT RATS (1939–45)

The British 8th Army comprised a mixture of British and Commonwealth forces that had been sent to the Middle East between 1939 and 1941. Collectively they were dubbed the 'Desert Rats', as their war was waged surrounded by sand. By November 1941, when Operation Crusader was launched, the 8th Army was effectively two British Corps, the XIII and XXX. Specifically, these were the 7th Armoured, the South African 1st and 2nd, the Indian 4th, the New Zealand 2nd and elements of the 1st Armoured and 5th Indian divisions. Prior to this campaign the British 70th Infantry and 2nd Armoured Division had served in Egypt and Libya, along with the Australian 6th and 9th Divisions. As the campaign in North Africa developed, the 8th Army acquired X Corps, which consisted of the 8th and 10th Armoured Divisions, the 44th, 50th and 51st Infantry Divisions and the 10th Indian Division, plus several other smaller armoured units. The Desert Rats were exclusively British and Commonwealth and at no time contained either US or French troops.

◖ *see* Second Battle of El Alamein p. 181

BATTLE OF STALINGRAD (15 SEPTEMBER 1942–2 FEBRUARY 1943)

The Russian defence of Stalingrad was both determined and ferocious, despite massive air attacks and ground assaults; they stubbornly held and contested every inch of the city, resulting in bitter house-to-house fighting. Towards the end of September the Russians launched a series of counterattacks on the flanks of Stalingrad and the Germans were forced to find additional reserves. By the beginning of October German impetus had petered out and by 11 October, after 51 days of fighting, they had made little forward movement. On 14 October Russian reserves were moved into position but four days later the Germans renewed their assault. On 18 November the Russians launched a huge offensive; they

▲ *ABOVE: Building debris on the outskirts of the besieged city of Stalingrad.*

threatened to cut the Germans off in Stalingrad by attacking the weaker flanks. Within four days 250,000 Germans had been trapped. The German commander Paulus made desperate attempts to break out and outside attempts to break in failed. By 31 January Paulus was forced to seek surrender terms and two days later 90,000 survivors began their march to captivity in Siberia. German deaths numbered 160,000; only 34,000 were successfully evacuated from Stalingrad by air.

◆ *see* Siege of Leningrad p. 120

SECOND BATTLE OF EL ALAMEIN (23 OCTOBER–5 NOVEMBER 1942)

The second Battle of El Alamein was in fact two operations masterminded by General Montgomery. The first, Operation Lightfoot, opened at 21:30 on 23 October 1942; it saw the greatest concentration of Allied artillery so far in the war. Montgomery had an advantage of 2:1 in men, tanks and aircraft. Characteristically, however, the Germans reacted swiftly. Rommel did not reach the battlefield until 25 October, but he immediately launched a series of counterattacks. Although ground had been made, Montgomery's first operation had been thwarted. He launched a second major offensive, Operation Supercharge, at 01:00 on 2 November. This time his armour managed to penetrate the minefields and by the evening Rommel had just 32 tanks left in action. Rommel now faced disaster: his Italian support troops were being wiped out and despite Hitler's express instructions that he should not retreat, he ordered a withdrawal on 4 November. Heavy rains on 7 November allowed Rommel to extricate many of his men from the battlefield. The British advance continued, Tobruk fell on 13 November followed by Benghazi on 20 November. The race to overrun Libya and Tunisia was now on.

⬦ see Bernard Montgomery p. 182

MONTGOMERY, BERNARD (1887–1976)

Montgomery began his military career in 1908, serving in India and on the Western Front during World War I. He remained in the army during the interwar years, reaching the rank of Major-General by 1938.

In June 1940, he extricated his 2nd Corps from France via Dunkirk and was given several UK-based commands until July 1942. Montgomery was then offered command of the 8th Army in Egypt to face Rommel. On 23 October 1942 he launched Operation Lightfoot, which failed to meet its objectives; on 1 November, however, his Operation Supercharge broke through the

▶ *RIGHT: British commander Bernard Montgomery.*

German and Italian lines, recapturing Tobruk and Tripoli, and forcing the Axis surrender in North Africa.

Montgomery was instrumental in the invasion of Sicily and the Italian mainland (July–October 1943), and in command of all ground troops for D-Day (Operation Overlord) in June 1944. He also masterminded Operation Market Garden in September 1944.

In 1945 Montgomery became Commander of the British occupation troops in Germany and later Deputy Supreme Commander of Allied forces in Europe, under General Eisenhower. He died on 25 March 1976.

◆ *see* Second Battle of El Alamein p. 181

OPERATION TORCH (8–11 NOVEMBER 1942)

Operation Torch, the planned invasion of Vichy-held north-west Africa by Allied troops, witnessed a vast amphibious landing that significantly involved US troops. Although Torch would be overshadowed by Operation Overlord in 1944, it was nonetheless an overwhelming show of force. Landings began around 01:00 on 8 November 1942 and, in a politically sensitive situation, Frenchmen were forced to fight their compatriots. Vichy troops initially showed determined opposition. At 07:00 Pétain received a letter from Roosevelt, imploring him to throw his support behind the Anglo-American invasion. Pétain passed the decision to his High Commissioner in Algiers, but outwardly assured the Germans of his support. By 11 November it had become clear to the Vichy authorities that continued resistance would be useless and at 07:00 the ceasefire came into force. On the same day German troops marched into unoccupied France. Germany realized that the Vichy French had no stomach to fight the Allies. The occupation went ahead, despite Pétain's protests; German troops were now landing at Tunis.

◆ *see* British Enter Libya and Tunisia p. 187

1943

CASABLANCA CONFERENCE (14–24 JANUARY 1943)

Although only Roosevelt and Churchill amongst the big three leaders were able to attend the Casablanca Conference, the Russians were represented by key officials. Stalin was adamant that the Anglo-Americans should open a second front in Europe, arguing that Germany would surely crumble if it faced a war on two fronts. While Roosevelt supported a French landing, Churchill preferred Italy, describing it as the 'soft underbelly of Europe'. This would also give the Allies the opportunity to link up with Russian troops in the Balkans. In return for agreeing to an invasion of France in 1944, Roosevelt committed to landings in Sicily and Italy as soon as was practicable. Meanwhile, the Allied air fleets would concentrate on destroying German industry, with unconditional surrender the only outcome.

◆ *see* Roosevelt, Churchill and Stalin Meet at Teheran p. 210

STURMOVIK (1940–45)

The Sturmovik, deployed by the Germans in World War II, was generally used as a ground-support aircraft, although other variants were constructed that would eventually carry torpedoes and could be used in aerial attacks. The first mass-produced Sturmovik was available by the time the Germans invaded Russia. They were effective in their role, but casualties of the aircraft and pilots were extremely high. The improved version first appeared on the battlefield on 30 October 1942. The aircraft was heavily armoured in comparison with the German aircraft it would face and it became the most feared Russian aircraft on the Eastern Front. It was cheap and straightforward to manufacture and consequently over 36,000 were built. It had four 20-mm canons, two machine guns and could carry around 1,000 kg of bombs. Its canons were capable of penetrating virtually any German tank. Vast numbers roamed the battlefields, making daytime movement extremely hazardous.

see Warsaw Ghetto p. 194

BRITISH ENTER LIBYA AND TUNISIA (23 JANUARY 1943)

In the three months after the El Alamein offensive by Montgomery's 8th Army, Allied troops entered the last Italian-held city of Mussolini's North African empire. The 11th Hussars arrived in Tripoli at dawn on 23 January and by noon the Union Jack had been set flying over the central square. Ten days previously, General Leclerc's Free French had joined Montgomery's men and driven across the Tunisian border in pursuit of Rommel's Afrika Korps.

see Kasserine Pass p. 191

LEFT: General Giraud, Roosevelt, de Gaulle and Churchill at the Casablanca Conference.

USAAF TARGETS GERMANY (27 JANUARY 1943)

The attack on the German warehousing and industrial plant at Wilhelmshaven by the US 8th Air Force was the air raid that set the pattern for operations over the next 18 months. Over 60 B-17s and B-24s hit Wilhemshaven, while others attacked Copenhagen and Dusseldorf. To coincide with broadcasts by Goering and Goebbels – who stated German victory as assured – the RAF made daylight attacks on Berlin and saturation attacks on Hamburg.

see The Dambusters p. 195

◄ *LEFT: US Flying Fortresses.*

THE CHINDITS (1943–45)

The Chindits, named after the mythical 'Chinthe' beasts that guard Burmese temples, was a multi-national force led by Orde C Wingate. The 77th Brigade consisted of the 13th King's (Liverpool) Regiment, the 3rd Battalion 2nd Gurkha Rifles, the Burmese Rifles and the 142nd Commando Group – 3,000 men in total. Wingate's tactics were revolutionary: he split troops into mixed columns of 300, each led by a major, which contained a cross-section of all arms. These columns terrorized the Japanese in Burma and specialized in hit-and-run missions. The first mission occurred on 14–15 February 1943 at the Chindwin River at Tonhe and Auktaung respectively. The operation lasted two months; they penetrated beyond the Irawaddy into Japanese-held Burma. By 4 February 1944 there were six brigades and they began their march from India to Indaw in Burma, establishing airstrips and ensuring supplies. From 17 March to 10 May the main Chindit base, 'White City', saw immense pressure from the Japanese. With the support of No. 7 Air Commando, the seemingly impossible had been achieved. At the height of the operations they were supplying and supporting 14 British, five Gurkha, three West African and two Burmese battalions, amounting to some 20,000 troops.

◻ *see* Orde Wingate p. 189

ORDE WINGATE (1903–44)

Wingate was a British career soldier. He was first commissioned in 1923, and served five years in the Sudan Defence Force (1928–33). Wingate joined the intelligence staff in Palestine in 1936, was wounded in action against Arab fighters in July 1938. In 1939 he was sent to

▲ *ABOVE: Wingate's guerillas.*

command Gideon Force in the Sudan and led attacks on Italian-held Abyssinia, causing 12,000 enemy troops to surrender to a fraction of that number of British troops. Wingate was then posted to India, where he formed the Chindits. His first operation took place in February 1943, and he later met Churchill and Roosevelt to explain his strategies against the Japanese. Wingate's major offensive began on 14 March 1944, with the Chindits operating 322 km (200 miles) behind Japanese lines. Wingate's men managed to cut an airstrip out of the jungle for re-supply and over the next few months caused immense damage to the Japanese throughout Burma. Wingate had planned to disrupt the Japanese to assist the offensive actions by Stilwell in the north and Slim's attacks on Imphal and Kohima. Losses were high and the casualties included Wingate himself, who died when his aircraft went down near Imphal during a storm on 14 March 1944.

◨ *see* The Chindits p. 189

MERRILL'S MARAUDERS (1943–44)

In August 1943 volunteers formed a group to carry out Project Galahad. It required experienced jungle fighters and by late October 3,000 men had reported to the unit's base in Bombay. In January 1944 the unit was given the designation 5307th Composite Unit (Provisional) and placed under the command of Brigadier General Frank Merrill. Although in existence only until August 1944, they fought 35 battles against the Japanese, with one particularly celebrated action on 28 March 1944. Their objectives were Shaduzup and Inkangahtawng but the group were forced to withdraw towards Hsamshingyang, pursued by Japanese. At 10:30 on 28 March the marauders had reached Nhpum Ga with little time before the Japanese would close. By 31 March the American garrison was isolated and for the next 10 days the Japanese launched increasingly ferocious attacks on Nhpum Ga. Japanese casualties were mounting and the pressure from the other two American battalions was increasing. Merrill had suffered from a heart attack and Colonel Charles Hunter took over command. They pushed towards Nhpum Ga from 3 April and by 6 April they had made some headway and met light resistance. In the whole operation the 2nd had lost 25 men and claimed 400 Japanese dead.

◘ see Behind Enemy Lines p. 221

KASSERINE PASS (14–25 FEBRUARY 1943)

The Battle of Kasserine Pass was both an attempt by Rommel to take pressure off Tunisia and a baptism of fire for US ground troops in the Western Theatre. At 04:00 on 14 February 1943 German troops attempted to break through the Allied lines in the direction of Kasserine. If successful, further offensives would be launched to support it. Initially German troops made headway, but Montgomery's 8th Army was pushing up on the Mareth Line. On 18 February German troops took Sbeitla, but by 22 February, with British troops arriving to support the Americans, Rommel began to break off the attacks. Two days later Allied troops re-entered Kasserine. Allied casualties had topped 10,000, half of which were American. The last German offensive had cost them 2,000.

◘ see Fall of Tunis p. 194

BATTLE OF THE BISMARCK SEA (3–5 MARCH 1943)

Eight Japanese transport ships, escorted by eight destroyers en route to New Guinea, were intercepted by US aircraft. The Japanese commander had been relying on air cover, but American and Australian aircraft had pounded Japanese airfields and then tackled the invasion fleet. All the Japanese transports were sunk as well as four of the destroyers; 3,500 Japanese were lost. It was an important tactical victory for General MacArthur.

◘ *see* Operation Vengeance p. 193

FAILED ASSASSINATION ATTEMPT ON HITLER (13 MARCH 1943)

Henning von Tresckow was a senior German army officer who had fought on the Eastern Front between 1941 and the middle of 1943. He led a conspiracy to assassinate Hitler – an elaborate attempt that involved placing a bomb on Hitler's aircraft when it left Smolensk on 13 March. The attempt failed but von Tresckow remained undetected and after the July plot failure, committed suicide.

◘ *see* Adolf Hitler p. 54

◄ *LEFT: Hitler with a plaster on his hand after the failed attempt on his life by Henning von Tresckow.*

OPERATION VENGEANCE (18 APRIL 1943)

Having intercepted Japanese ciphers and radio messages, US forces became aware that Admiral Yamamoto would be en route to Bougainville on 18 April. Yamamoto was the architect of the Pearl Harbor attack and Operation Vengeance was set in motion when US P-38s of the 13th Air Force left Guadalcanal and shot down Yamamoto's aircraft over Bougainville. It was a crippling strategic and moral loss for the Japanese, but a considerable morale booster for America.

◆ *see* Isokoru Yamamoto p. 193

YAMAMOTO, ISOKORU (1884–1943)

Yamamoto was a Japanese career naval officer who had served as an ensign during the Russo-Japanese War. In the 1930s he masterminded the transition of the Japanese fleets, notably the building of aircraft carriers and the development of naval aviation. He became the Minister of the Navy in 1938 and proposed the plan to make a pre-emptive strike on the US fleet at Pearl Harbor in 1941. Yamamoto organized the invasions of the Solomon Islands and New Guinea, and in the summer of 1942 he attempted to capture Midway Island. The attack was an unmitigated disaster and Yamamoto lost four of his much-prized aircraft carriers. From this point, Yamamoto was on the back foot and his attempts to prevent the US from taking Guadalcanal (November 1942) failed. The US intercepted Japanese signals indicating that Yamamoto was to visit Bougainville in April 1943. They launched Operation Vengeance, in which US aircraft shot down Yamamoto's transport over Bougainville on 18 April 1943. Yamamoto's death was not officially reported by the Japanese until 21 May, by which time Mineichi Koga had taken his place.

◆ *see* Bougainville p. 199

WARSAW GHETTO (19 APRIL–16 MAY 1943)

The Warsaw ghetto was a vast city prison containing 400,000 Jews. In four weeks from 19 April 1943, SS troops and Gestapo units under the command of SS Brigadier-General Stroop, slaughtered over 56,000 men, women and children in the ghetto. Stroop would later claim that he had been working under orders from Hitler to eliminate the ghetto and its inhabitants. Although the ghetto dwellers had tried to resist, the 10-ft wall around them had cut them off from safety. The SS, Gestapo and Ukrainian troops were aided in the massacre by Jewish collaborators and policemen. Stroop himself was sentenced to death at an American court hearing in Dachau on 22 March 1947. Sentence was carried out by hanging at the scene of his crimes, Warsaw, on 8 September 1951.

see Oradour-Sur-Glane Massacre p. 236

FALL OF TUNIS (6–13 MAY 1943)

At dawn on 6 May 1943 the British 1st Army began its long-planned assault on Tunis. The British forces were supported to the south by French troops and to the north by US forces heading for Bizerta. Von Arnim had recently replaced Rommel as commander but he was powerless to stop the onslaught. At 15:40 on 7 May British troops entered Tunis, narrowly beating the US entry into Bizerta at 16:15. What remained of the Axis forces withdrew to the Cape Bon peninsular. Officially fighting ended at 11:00 on 9 May in north-east Tunisia, but the fighting continued over the following two days until finally Von Arnim surrendered to Montgomery, leading his 250,000 German and Italian troops into captivity. The war in North Africa was over.

see Operation Husky p. 198

TRIDENT CONFERENCE IN WASHINGTON (12–25 MAY 1943)

The Trident Conference approved the plans for Operation Husky – the landings in Sicily that were scheduled for 10 July. A date was also set for Operation Overlord (the D-day landings), with a provisional date of May 1944. The first target, however, would be Italy, with the aim of knocking the country out of the war. The outline strategy in the Pacific was also approved.

◆ *see* Operation Overlord p. 229

THE DAMBUSTERS (16 MAY 1943)

No. 617 Squadron was formed at Scampton in March 1943 to launch Operation Chastise, the bombing and breeching of three vital dams in the Ruhr region. The mission was led by Guy Gibson, who was given permission to poach any Lancaster crew he felt suitable for the job. The attack required low-level precision

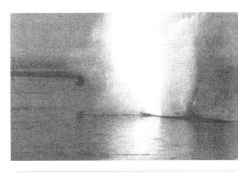

▲ *ABOVE: A 'bouncing bomb'.*

bombing over water and for weeks not even Gibson was told what the target would be. The bomb, designed by Barnes Wallace, was a mine that had to be dropped at exactly 18 m (60 ft), at a speed of 354 kph (220 mph). Nineteen Lancasters were modified to carry out the attack, which was scheduled for 16–17 May. Each of the bombs weighed 4.5 tons; the targets were the Mohne, the Eder and the Sorpe dams. These provided 75 per cent of the electrical power for German industry in the Ruhr basin. The Mohne and the Eder dams were successfully destroyed, but eight aircraft were lost during the raid. The Germans managed to repair the dams quickly and the Ruhr area was soon back in production. The raid was one of the most audacious operations of the war, proving that no German target was too difficult to deter the Allies from attempting its destruction.

see Guy Gibson p. 196

GIBSON, GUY (1918–44)

Gibson joined the RAF in 1936, winning the Distinguished Flying Cross in July 1940 during Bomber Command's first raid of the war. He then transferred to Fighter Command, where he scored four kills and added a bar to his DFC. In April 1942 he transferred back to Bomber Command – having been promoted to the rank of Wing Commander at the age of just 23 – and flew 172 missions as Commander of 106 Squadron, before being posted as Commander of 617 Squadron.

In February 1943 it was decided to launch an attack on the Ruhr dams and Gibson was selected to lead the raid. On the night of 16 May 1943, Gibson led 19 Lancasters, each one carrying a single bouncing bomb designed by Barnes Wallis, on the successful attack. Gibson was awarded the Victoria Cross for his role in the mission.

▶ RIGHT: Dambuster leader Guy Gibson.

In June 1944, Gibson returned to active duty after a lecture tour in the US and the writing of his book Enemy Coast Ahead. On 14 September 1944 he flew a Mosquito fighter bomber on a raid against German targets in Holland. He and his navigator were killed when their aircraft crashed over enemy territory.

◆ see Hamburg Raids p. 200

OPERATION CITADEL (5–16 JULY 1943)

The Germans launched their last major offensive in the east, Operation Citadel (the Battle of Kursk) on 5 July 1943. The engagement would take place on a 322-km (200-mile) front. On the south side of a vast salient the Germans had massed 2,000 tanks, including many of their new Panthers and Tigers. The Russians were heavily dug in with up to seven defensive lines. The assault began at 07:00, covered by 2,000 German aircraft. There was ferocious combat; collectively the engagement involved 6,000 tanks, 4,000 aircraft and two million men. Tank casualties in particular were extreme. With the numbers of dead and wounded mounting, the German assaults began to peter out and on 12 July the Russians went on the offensive. The Germans withdrew; Operation Citadel had failed.

◆ see The Tigers p. 197

THE TIGERS (1941–45)

Before May 1941, the Germans considered their lighter tanks adequate in battlefield actions, but after encountering the Matilda or the Russian T34s they realized they were poorly armoured and began planning production of a vehicle with 100-mm armour and a gun capable of penetrating that depth of armour from the distance of one mile. The Tiger I, as it became known, was the most powerful tank of its time, although it could not spearhead armour attacks as it was too slow and cumbersome. In August 1942, Hitler ordered the Army Weapons Office to develop a heavier tank, with 150-mm frontal armour capable of carrying the 8.8-cm gun, with sloping armour. The Tiger II was authorized for production in February 1944, with a new and simpler designed turret. In the autumn of 1944, German tank production was rationalized and the Tiger II and the Panther remained the only two turreted tanks to be kept in production for 1945. By March of that year, Tiger II production had fallen. The Tiger II was first encountered by Russian troops in May 1944 and on the Western Front in August. The Tiger II resembled a larger, up-gunned Panther with all of the punch of a Tiger I.

◆ *see* Russian Winter Offensive p. 210

OPERATION HUSKY (10 JULY 1943)

The long-awaited invasion of Europe – codenamed Operation Husky – began with Allied landings in Sicily on 10 July 1943. One hundred and sixty thousand men and 600 tanks were deployed against an estimated 300,000 Italians and 90,000 Germans. The landings were preceded by raids from Special

◀ *LEFT: The 'Tiger' tank.*

198

Forces. The following day Italian and German units launched a counterattack. Although the Italians were beaten off easily, the Germans proved tougher opposition and their tanks managed to penetrate to within a mile of the landing beaches. Meanwhile, British troops, having landed at Syracuse, drove up the coast to Augusta. By 12 July, two days after the operation was launched, the majority of German and Italian forces were withdrawing northwards. The foothold on Sicily had been achieved; the Americans alone had taken 18,000 prisoners. The race for Messina was now on.

🔷 *see* Race for Messina p. 200

BOUGAINVILLE (17 JULY 1943–24 MARCH 1944)

The battle for Bougainville began with a naval engagement between the US and Japanese fleets on 17 July 1943 and the fighting would fluctuate in intensity for many months. The last large-scale action took place on 24 March 1944, when a massive American counterattack succeeding in halting the Japanese, although skirmishing would continue as late as May.

🔷 *see* Tarawa p. 209

MUSSOLINI IS CENSURED AND IMPRISONED (24–25 JULY 1943)

The meeting of the Fascist Grand Council took place while Allied troops were wrestling control of Sicily on 24 July 1943. Italy had already lost North Africa and hundreds of thousands of men. It was now time for a regime change and Mussolini lost the vote of confidence. The following day the Italian leader was arrested and imprisoned. He was replaced by Badoglio, who determined that Italy would continue the war. The Germans immediately sent eight divisions south.

🔷 *see* Skorzeny Snatches Mussolini p. 206

HAMBURG RAIDS (24–28 JULY 1943)

On 24 July 1943 the RAF made a massive night raid on Hamburg, dropping 2,300 tons of bombs. At 08:00 the following morning Berlin radio reported 'all Hamburg seems to be in flames'. Indeed it was – 20,000 people had been killed and 60,000 seriously injured. The RAF had employed some 740 bombers and had used tinfoil strips to confuse the German radar systems. The US would add their weight on 25–26 July. Waves of bombers continued to pound the city; it was estimated that around 200,000 civilian deaths were caused by the time the raids ended. Even the roads were alight as the asphalt melted in the heat of the fires. This was the heaviest raid suffered so far by Germany.

see Operation Tidalwave p. 200

OPERATION TIDALWAVE (1 AUGUST 1943)

In line with the agreements made at the Trident Conference, Operation Tidalwave was launched on 1 August 1943. One hundred and seventy-seven B-24 Liberators of the US 9th Air Force hit Romanian oil fields, knocking out 40 per cent of their production capacity. The costs were high and 54 of the aircraft together with 232 air crew were lost. The Ploesti oil refineries would continue to be a target for the Allies.

see Operation Double Strike p. 202

RACE FOR MESSINA (12–17 AUGUST 1943)

With German and Italian forces in retreat, the British and Americans stepped up the pressure to be the first to reach Messina, at the north-eastern tip of Sicily. Ultimately, the US 3rd Division would claim the prize at 10:15 on 17 August. The capture of the whole island had taken 39 days, but the majority of the Germans – some 60,000 – had escaped to the mainland with their equipment.

see George Patton p. 201

PATTON, GEORGE (1885–1945)

Patton was a controversial US military commander, West Point graduate, Olympic athlete, pilot, horseman and tank commander. His association with tanks began during World War I and by October 1940 Patton was commanding the 2nd Armoured Division. His baptism took place in November 1942 when his troops invaded North Africa. By the time of the Sicily landings, he was commanding the 7th Army, taking Palermo (22 July 1943) and cutting off 50,000 Italian troops. Patton was implicated in the murder of over 70 Italian prisoners of war, an association which remained with him throughout his career. Patton was apt to handle his 'malingerers' forcibly and after several incidents he was replaced in January 1944. Patton was back in command in France in August 1944, however, staging the Allied breakout which reached the River Meuse on 30 August.

Patton's troops destroyed German resistance after their failed Ardennes offensive in December 1944 and his troops crossed the Rhine on 22 March 1945. Patton was made Governor of Bavaria, but he permitted former Nazis to remain in their positions of authority. Following a disastrous press conference, in September he was removed from office and posted to the 15th Army. He died from injuries received in a traffic accident on 21 December 1945.

 *see* Italy Surrenders p. 204

▶ *RIGHT: US general George Patton.*

OPERATION DOUBLE STRIKE (17 AUGUST 1943)

Operation Double Strike saw the first major US daylight raid over Germany. Their targets were the aircraft factories at Schweinfurt and Regensburg. Some 229 B-17s were deployed in the raid, which succeeded in seriously damaging the industrial areas of the two towns. The losses were high, however, and around 36 aircraft failed to return to their bases. A larger raid was planned for 14 October, a day that became known as Black Thursday. Four days before Operation Double Strike, 500 tons of bombs were dropped on Rome in order to persuade the new Italian government to surrender. Over 260 aircraft were employed from the 12th Air Force; the raid caused serious damage to the Italian capital.

RAF BOMBS PEENEMÜNDE (17 AUGUST 1943)

During the night of 17–18 August 1943, nearly 600 RAF bombers struck the V1 and V2 factories at Peenemünde, the central production centre for the Doodlebugs and the new V2 rocket being developed by Werner von Braun. Some 1,500 tons of explosives and incendiaries were dropped in the hope that the raid would stop, or at the very least seriously cripple, the continued construction and development of German rocket technology. The Peenemünde raid, occurring on the same day as the fall of Messina, proved a temporary respite for German cities, but a renewed Anglo-American bomber offensive would soon rain thousands more tons of bombs on Germany industry and civilian targets.

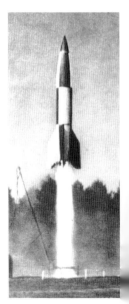

◆ see Werner von Braun p. 203

BRAUN, WERNER VON (1912–77)

Braun's involvement in rocket technology brought him to the attention of
Walter Dornberger – the man in charge of rocket research for the
German army – in 1932. Together the two men successfully developed two
rockets which were capable of flights of up to 2.4 km (1.5 miles). Braun
joined Dornberger at Peenemünde in 1937 in order to develop long-range
missiles; it was these that would eventually lead to the creation of the V2.

The V2 was first used in September 1944 – but not before Himmler
had temporarily arrested Braun on the accusation that he was more
interested in space flight than in the war effort. From September 1944
onwards, over 5,000 V2s were fired at Great Britain, with a little over 20
per cent of them reaching their targets. By March 1945 the launch sites
had been overrun and Braun fled west and surrendered to US forces.

Braun and 40 of his staff were shipped to the US to work on the
nuclear programme. In 1952 Braun became the technical director of the
US Ballistic Missile Agency and in 1960 the director of Marshall Space
Flight Center. Braun resigned and went into private industry in 1972; he
died on 16 June 1977.

see German Rocket Programme p. 271

ROOSEVELT AND CHURCHILL MEET IN QUEBEC (17–24 AUGUST 1943)

Roosevelt and Churchill confirmed their agreement of the launching of
Operation Overlord for May 1944, but for the time being they agreed to give
priority to Operation Pointblank, whose aim was to cripple German industry.
They also approved the invasion of the Italian mainland and drew out the
strategies that would be employed in the Pacific against the Japanese.
Mountbatten was placed in command of the South-East Asia front.

see Operation Overlord p. 229

◀ *LEFT: A German V2 rocket being launched at Peenemünde.*

ALLIES LAND IN SOUTHERN ITALY (3 SEPTEMBER 1943)

At 04:30 on 3 September 1943, Montgomery's 8th Army landed on mainland Italy. This was essentially a diversionary attack, as the main landings would take place at Salerno, but they met with little resistance. At 17:50 the same day, on the island of Sicily, Castellano signed an armistice on behalf of Badoglio. Italy would be out of the war in less than a week.

see Italy Surrenders p. 204

▲ ABOVE: US troops landing on the beach in Italy.

ITALY SURRENDERS (8 SEPTEMBER 1943)

Developments in Italy were occurring at a rapid pace. The 8th Army was driving inland and on 8 September Operation Avalanche, the main Allied landings in Italy, took place at Salerno. The troops began wading ashore at 17:30, coinciding with an announcement by Eisenhower that the Italians had made an unconditional surrender. At 21:45 Badoglio confirmed the statement, as Germans concentrated their troops to deal with the Salerno landings. The full landings took place at 03:30 on 9 September and British paratroops launched Operation Slapstick, capturing Taranto. Already there was widespread fighting between Italian troops and the Germans, who were by now moving in on Rome. The Italian royal family had fled to Brindisi. Hitler broke the news to the German population on 10 September.

◄► *see* Skorzeny Snatches Mussolini p. 206

GERMANS SEIZE ROME (10 SEPTEMBER 1943)

Following the sudden capitulation of Italy, German troops seized Rome on 10 September after skirmishes with Italian troops. Elsewhere, Montgomery was holding a line from Catanzaro to Nicastro and on 11 September the British 1st Airborne Division took Brindisi. Already German troops were moving to consolidate their positions; there were over a million Italian troops on the mainland and just 400,000 Germans. The German position was becoming increasingly precarious.

◄► *see* Albert Kesselring p. 205

KESSELRING, ALBERT (1881–1960)

Kesselring, a Major-General from 1932 and friend of Goering, was a member of the Luftwaffe and in 1936 became Goering's Chief of Staff. Kesselring commanded the 1st Air Fleet in the Polish campaign and the 2nd in the invasions of France, Belgium and Holland in 1940. Transferred to the Mediterranean the following year, and ultimately North Africa, he worked alongside Rommel. In November 1942 he was appointed Deputy Commander of Italian forces, but could not hold Tunisia or Sicily. Throughout 1943 his troops in Italy maintained a solid defence against the Allies.

▲ *ABOVE: Albert Kesselring.*

On October 25 1944 Kesselring was injured in a traffic accident and had to retire. He was captured by the Allies on 6 May 1945, tried and condemned to death. He was was granted a reprive on the grounds of ill-health and released in 1952. He died on 11 July 1960.

 see Cephalonia Massacre p. 207

SKORZENY SNATCHES MUSSOLINI (12 SEPTEMBER 1943)

Otto Skorzeny was the man who masterminded Mussolini's rescue from prison at Gran Sasso. Skorzeny's men slipped out of Rome and headed for Gaeta on 27 July, sailing for Ponza the following day, after receiving intelligence that Mussolini was on Sardinia. By 20 August he had formulated his plan. The rescue was scheduled to take place on 27 August, but Mussolini had been moved. Skorzeny re-planned the move for 12 September. His men landed in a glider and the Italian guards were so shocked they didn't fire at them. Skorzeny's men charged into the rooms and the Italians fled; so far no one had fired a shot. With great difficulty Mussolini was manoeuvred into a light aircraft and packed off to Rome, where he boarded another aircraft bound for Vienna.

 see Benito Mussolini p. 206

MUSSOLINI, BENITO (1883–1945)

Corporal Mussolini was wounded in World War I, then entered Italian politics, organizing right-wing groups in the Fascist Party and rising to power in 1922. By 1929 Italy had become a one-party state; Mussolini was popular, carrying out reforms and public works programmes. In 1935, he ordered the invasion of Ethiopia, gaining control by the summer of 1936.

In 1939 he signed a military alliance with Germany. Italy entered the war on 10 June 1940, fighting in North Africa and in Egypt. Disasters in North Africa and Greece made Italy dependent on Germany by late 1941.

When Sicily fell (July 1943), Mussolini's position was undermined and on 24 July he was ousted and arrested. On 12 September, Otto Skorzeny – on orders from Hitler – freed Mussolini and he set up a rival government in northern Italy. By May 1944, German resistance was crumbling in Italy, Rome fell on 4 June followed by Florence on 12 August.

The British 8th Army crossed the River Po on 23 April 1945, signalling partisan uprisings in Milan and Genoa. Mussolini and his mistress attempted fleeing to

▲ *ABOVE: Italian leader Benito Mussolini.*

Switzerland, but were captured near Lake Como on 27 April 1945; they were shot in Milan and their bodies displayed as a warning to others.

◆ *see* Monte Cassino p. 216

CEPHALONIA MASSACRE (13–26 SEPTEMBER 1943)

On 8 September 1943, the new Italian government officially announced the cessation of hostilities against the Allies. For the 12,000-strong Italian garrison on the Greek island of Cephalonia, this presented problems. The Italians, commanded by Russian Front veteran, Antonio Gaudin, fought pitched battles with German forces under Major von Hirschfeld, supported by Stuka dive bombers. After the Italian surrender, the Germans shot 4,750 of the men; a further 3,000 died when the transport ships heading for Germany hit mines. In all over 10,000 Italians were killed. Von Hirschfeld was later killed in action in Warsaw, but Hubert Lonz, another German commander, was sentenced to 12 years at Nuremberg.

◆ *see* Skorzeny Snatches Mussolini p. 206

ITALY DECLARES WAR ON GERMANY (13 OCTOBER 1943)

▲ *ABOVE: Italy surrenders to the Allies.*

At 15:00 on 13 October Badoglio completed the Italian about-face by declaring war on Germany. He urged Italian soldiers to resist the Germans to the last man. In truth Badoglio had little option, with overwhelming Allied forces already in Italy and the Germans carrying out widespread looting. All across the country Germans were taking reprisals against Italians and there were random shootings and destruction of buildings – even hospitals had been attacked.

◆ *see* Monte Cassino p. 216

BLACK THURSDAY (14 OCTOBER 1943)

Following the 17 August raid against Schweinfurt, US aircraft of the 8th Air Force, launched another attack on the ball-bearing factories. Some 300 aircraft were involved in the raid, which occurred unescorted in daylight. US Air Force casualties were enormous and 60 of the aircraft were shot down, with 138 badly damaged. This raid, known as Black

Thursday because of the severity of the losses, had in fact achieved very little and the ball-bearing factories had hardly been touched. Daylight raids would continue in ever-increasing intensity and on 3 November, 500 US 8th Air Force bombers devastated Wilhelmshafen Harbour in one such mission. The sheer weight of numbers would eventually turn the air war against the Germans.

see USAAF Seizes Command of the Air p. 214

KIEV LIBERATED (6 NOVEMBER 1943)

On 4 November 1943 Russian troops had created a bridgehead on the River Dneipr and threatened to surround Kiev. By the following day German troops were indeed in grave danger of being surrounded. On 6 November they withdrew, leaving behind them the wreckage of Kiev's most beautiful buildings, but the third largest city in Russia was back in friendly hands. The Russians pursued, but were held at Fastov by stubborn resistance.

see Russian Winter Offensive p. 210

TARAWA (20 NOVEMBER–23 DECEMBER 1943)

One of the key targets of Operation Galvanic was the atolls of Tarawa and Makin in the Gilbert Islands. Tarawa was held by 5,000 Japanese and from the moment the first wave of US marines hit the beaches, at 08:25 on 20 November, they came under intense fire. On 21 November more marines were deployed. Casualties in the hand-to-hand fighting were enormous on both sides, with neither asking for nor receiving quarter. Finally, on 23 November, the two atolls fell. On Makin the Japanese had lost 450 for just 64 Americans, but on Tarawa all but 17 of the 5,000-strong Japanese garrison had been killed. The following day 700 more US troops died when the *Liscome Bay* was sunk by a Japanese submarine.

see Operation Dexterity p. 210

ROOSEVELT, CHURCHILL AND STALIN MEET AT TEHERAN (28–30 NOVEMBER 1943)

Stalin, Roosevelt and Churchill met in Teheran for a conference code named Eureka. Utmost priority was given to Operation Overlord and Anvil, which would be an Allied landing in southern France. Stalin undertook to join in the war against Japan as soon as the Germans were beaten. No sooner had the meeting dispersed, it was reconvened between December 3 and 7 in Cairo, where more detailed planning continued. Proposed operations to recapture Burma were cancelled to give priority to Operation Anvil. It was proposed that January 1944 be the date for the invasion of the Marshall Islands and New Britain. New Guinea would be recaptured by June and the Mariana Islands liberated by October 1944.

▶ *see* Yalta Conference p. 276

OPERATION DEXTERITY (15 DECEMBER 1943)

Operation Dexterity was the codename for the Australian-American amphibious landing in New Britain. The landing was completed by 07:00 on 15 December and Japanese resistance was swiftly overcome. Various outlying islands fell the next day and the Japanese tried to resist by throwing aircraft at the invasion fleet, but met with little success. By 24 December US bombers were ranging far and wide, hitting Japanese targets at will across all of New Britain.

▶ *see* Marshall Islands p. 219

RUSSIAN WINTER OFFENSIVE (24 DECEMBER 1943)

Although the Russians had launched an offensive on the Ukrainian front on 10 December, the major blow took place in the Kiev area, with six armies and three assault groups hitting the German Army Group

▲ ABOVE: Stalin, Roosevelt and Churchill meet at the Teheran Conference.

South. The Germans resisted as best they could, but the Russians quickly took key positions and began pressing forward. By 26 December over 150 Russian towns and villages had been liberated. By 31 December Vitebsk was virtually surrounded and by 2 January 1944 they were just 29 km (18 miles) from the original Polish border. They were encountering stiffer German opposition, but on 7 January the Russians broke through once again and surged westward, on a 97-km (60-mile) front, trapping large numbers of German troops behind them.

◆ see Battle of the Dniepr p. 220

1944

USAAF SEIZES CONTROL OF THE AIR (11 JANUARY 1944)

In January 1944, the US Air Force received a vital addition to its armoury in the form of the P-51 Mustang. This fighter aircraft and interceptor had the capacity to accompany US bombers all the way to their targets and back. This now meant that German aircraft could not interdict Allied daylight raids without running the risk of suffering huge casualties from these fast and highly manoeuvrable aircraft.

◆ see Lightning and Thunderbolt p. 214

LIGHTNING AND THUNDERBOLT (1939–45)

The P-38 Lightning was probably the most advanced aircraft of its time when it first flew on 27 January 1939. Its development, under the strictest secrecy, had cost Lockhead $6 billion. Its strength was its design, speed (666 kph/414 mph) and range (3,636 km/2,259 miles). The Lightning was a great all-round performer; it could out-run and out-distance the opposition. When it came into operation in 1942 it could beat anything put in the air by the Axis Powers.

The P-47 Thunderbolt was, however, the most famous US aircraft of the war, with over 15,600 built. It was originally conceived as an interceptor, but it was also used as a heavy fighter, high-altitude escort and a fighter bomber. It was delivered to the USAAF in March 1942 and made its first combat flight over Europe in April 1943. The Thunderbolt was a sturdy and rugged aircraft that would serve in all theatres for several Allied air forces.

The P-47D had a maximum speed of 689 kph (428 mph), a ceiling of 12,810 m (42,028 ft) and a range of 1,488 km (925 miles). In addition to six machine guns it was also capable of carrying a load of over 1,100 kg (usually bombs, rockets or extra fuel tanks).

◆ see Mustang p. 215

▲ ABOVE: The American plane 'Thunderbolt'.

MUSTANG (1942–53)

The Mustang (P-51) was originally designed at Britain's request and called the NA-73. The USAAF purchased some early versions for use as ground-support aircraft. It was then decided to fit the aircraft with the Rolls-Royce Merlin engine giving it a greater speed (703 kph/437 mph) and a higher ceiling altitude. The initial prototypes were built in 1942, but by 1943 they had entered service and combat over Europe. The Mustang became the ultimate high-altitude escort for the USAAF B-17 and B-24 bombers. Its role as interceptor (dealing with incoming German fighters) proved unbeatable and the aircraft accounted for nearly 5,000 German aircraft kills during the war. Mustangs also saw combat in other theatres, including the Pacific, where they escorted US bombers en route from Iwo Jima to Japan. In all, some 14,855 Mustangs were built during the war for the USAAF, staying in service until 1953.

In 1942, the RAF deployed 15 Mustang squadrons, mostly earlier versions of the aircraft; many were subsequently replaced by Spitfires or reduced to training aircraft as the war continued. The first enemy aircraft to fall to a Mustang was, fittingly, shot down by a plane piloted by an American serving in the RAF during the Dieppe raid.

◆ *see* Mustang p. 215

MONTE CASSINO (12 JANUARY–17 MAY 1944)

Monte Cassino, 161 km (100 miles) to the south-east of Rome, was the pivotal point on the German-held Gustav Line. It dominated the surrounding countryside. The Allies had bombed the town of Cassino as early as 10 September 1943, but by the time the Allies reached the area the Germans had dug in. The first Allied assault took place on 17 January 1944, to coincide with the Anzio landings. It was an abject disaster and a second assault was planned for 15 February. The attack

was preceded by an intense bombardment. New Zealand infantry seized the town, whilst US troops secured Snakeshead Hill. The third attack took place on 15 March, with Ghurkas, New Zealanders and Poles all involved in the assault. Cassino would not fall until 17 May.

▲ *ABOVE: A New Zealand soldier aiming his rifle during the attack on Monte Cassino.*

EISENHOWER BECOMES SUPREME COMMANDER (16 JANUARY 1944)

On 16 January 1944 General Dwight Eisenhower was appointed Supreme Commander of Allied invasion forces in Europe or more precisely, Head of Supreme Headquarters Allied Expeditionary Force (SHAEF). He would therefore be in place to oversee all European operations, including the proposed Operation Overlord and Anvil.

see Dwight D. Eisenhower p. 217

EISENHOWER, DWIGHT D. (1890–1969)

Prior to 1942, Eisenhower's military career had been less than impressive, yet in March he was sent to Britain as leader of the European Theatre of Operations. Eisenhower was given command of Operation Torch (8 November 1942), the Allied landings in north-west Africa. Supporting Montgomery's 8th Army, advancing from Egypt, Axis resistance was defeated by May 1943.

Eisenhower, now a full General, began organizing the invasion of Italy, beginning with Sicily (July 1943) then the mainland (September 1943). He was given the responsibility of organizing three million troops for the full invasion of Europe as Head of Supreme Headquarters Allied Expeditionary Force (SHAEF). Eisenhower continued in this role until the fall of Germany in 1945.

Eisenhower retired in 1948, but became Supreme Commander of NATO in 1951 and on 20 January 1953 became President of the United States. He oversaw the Korean War (1950–53) and was re-elected in 1956. When he finally left office, he concentrated on writing his memoirs, published between 1963 and 1967. Eisenhower, possibly one of the most popular US Presidents of all time, and the first soldier to become President since Ulysses S. Grant in 1869, died at Gettysburg on 28 March 1969.

see Anzio and the Fall of Rome p. 218

ANZIO AND THE FALL OF ROME (22 JANUARY–4 JUNE 1944)

Within 24 hours of the landings, codenamed Operation Shingle, 36,000 Allied troops reached within 48 km (30 miles) of Rome. They met little opposition and it seemed that the road to Rome was clear. Rather than causing the Germans severe difficulties and forcing them to abandon Rome, the vast army simply sat and waited for the Germans to come to them. As a result, Rome remained in German hands until 4 June, when elements of General Mark Clark's 9th Army entered the city. In truth, the Anzio landings, although they had been a singular failure, had drawn the bulk of the German troops to them, where they had been comprehensively defeated. Their demise would hasten the fall of Italy.

◈ see Operation Dragoon-Anvil p. 248

▲ *ABOVE: An American Sherman tank going ashore at Anzio in Italy.*

MARSHALL ISLANDS (30 JANUARY 1944)

Forty-thousand men were earmarked to deal with the 8,000 Japanese defenders of the Marshall Islands. The primary problem was that the 2,000 islands and islets extended some 998 km (620 miles) and had to be taken in order to push towards Japan. The Japanese had dug in on nearly all the major positions, and despite the fact that US aircraft had been pounding the islands and Japanese shipping for a considerable time, they were still to put up a fanatical defence. Based on previous experience, the islands were saturated with explosives before the marines landed. Even then many of the defenders had escaped certain death. Throughout the whole campaign every inch of every island would be contested in the most ferocious manner. Casualties would be high for both belligerents.

◊ see New Guinea p. 226

NIMITZ BECOMES GOVERNOR OF THE MARSHALL ISLANDS (4 FEBRUARY 1944)

In recognition that the struggle for the Marshall Islands would continue for some time, Chester Nimitz was placed in command of the operations. On the same day Japanese resistance on Kwajalein ceased, having cost the US 177 dead and 1,000 wounded. Some 4,800 Japanese had been killed or were missing and just 41 had been taken prisoner. Operations continued to proceed on other islands in the southern sectors.

◊ see Chester Nimitz p. 219

NIMITZ, CHESTER (1885–1966)

Nimitz was a career naval officer and expert on submarine warfare; by 1938 he was commanding surface fleets. After Pearl Harbor, assigned to the Pacific Fleet, he took offensive actions against the Marshall and Gilbert Islands. Nimitz was instrumental in causing the defeat of the Japanese navy in the Coral Sea and Midway. Nimitz worked with Douglas

LOOK

Our Coming Conquest of Japan

Westbrook Pegler-
TONIC OR POISON?

OCTOBER 17, 1944

6d

Admiral Chester W. Nimitz
(Page 23)

▲ ABOVE: Chester Nimitz.

MacArthur and King (Commander-in-Chief of the US Fleet), finding himself between these two leaders' differing opinions of how the Pacific War should be fought. Nimitz remained in command (appointed Fleet Admiral in December 1944) until replaced by Raymond Spruance. In November 1945 Nimitz replaced King. He retired in 1947 and became a functionary of the United Nations. He died at home in San Francisco on 20 February 1966.

◀▶ see New Guinea p. 226

BATTLE OF THE DNIEPR (6–9 FEBRUARY 1944)

On 6 February 1944 the Russians captured Apostolovo, a vital railroad junction between Krivoy Rog and Nikopol, and trapped five divisions of the German 6th Army. Over the next two days the Russians systematically annihilated the German bridgehead over the River Dneipr. It is believed that some 75,000 Germans perished in the action. Meanwhile, continued pressure on the rest of the front ensured the liberation of the Ukraine and the recapture of the Crimea by May 1944. On 17 February the Korsun-Shevchenkosky pocket was finally eliminated by the Russians. Estimates vary as to the German losses, which could not have been less than 55,000 dead and 18,200 taken prisoner. The victory was celebrated the following day with a 224-gun salute in Moscow.

◘ see Sevastopol is Liberated p. 227

TOJO BECOMES DICTATOR (21 FEBRUARY 1944)

General Hideki Tojo, the Japanese Prime Minister, assumed the position of the Chief of the Japanese Army General Staff, replacing Field Marshall Sugiyama, effectively making him the military dictator of Japan. Tojo took over at a time when Japanese forces were being forced back on all fronts. They were withdrawing in Burma, the Marshall Islands had fallen to the US, and Saipan, Tinian, Rota and Guam were all under air attack.

◘ see Hideki Tojo p. 121

BEHIND ENEMY LINES (MARCH 1944)

An integral part of the operations against the Japanese in Burma was the insertion of troops deep behind enemy lines. Amongst the most famous of the units involved were Merrill's Marauders

▲ ABOVE: Wingate's guerillas behind Japanese lines.

and the Chindits, who ranged far and wide across the jungles of Burma and beyond, attacking isolated Japanese positions, destroying their war materials and cutting their lines of communication. One of the most stunning operations occurred from March 1944, when Chindit units, directed by Mountbatten, established an air strip behind Japanese lines in Burma, precipitating a series of running battles in the jungle against the Japanese. Most of these operations took place at a time when the Japanese were still menacing India, but they would ultimately contribute to the Japanese failure.

see Joseph Stilwell p. 222

STILWELL, JOSEPH (1883–1946)

Stilwell was a West Point graduate, who had served in the Philippines and on the Western Front during World War I, before being posted to India in February 1942. He was to command US forces in China, Burma and India and convinced the Chinese leader, Chiang Kai-shek to let him take command of Chinese forces in Burma. When Allied forces retreated to India in May 1942, Stilwell marched with his men rather than abandon them. He was appointed Deputy Supreme Allied Commander under Mountbatten in August 1943. He launched a fresh offensive against Japanese-held Burma and assumed the role of Personnel Commander of Operations in December 1943. The Japanese launched their Ichi-Go offensive in China in 1944, overrunning US airfields in China. This time, Chiang Kai-shek blamed Stilwell for the reversals leading to Stilwells' recall to the US. Stilwell returned to active duty in order to clean up Japanese resistance in Okinawa (June 1945). He then took over as Governor of Okinawa, but was considered unsuitable for the post and recalled to Washington in October. Stilwell died on 12 October 1946, convinced to the last that he should have been given a more prominent role during the war.

◼ *see* War in China p. 123

ICHIGO OFFENSIVE (APRIL 1944–JULY 1944)

The Japanese launched a two-pronged offensive from April 1944. The first was aimed at Burma, but the Chinese part of the campaign made great strides against the Chinese Nationalists led by Chiang Kai-shek and destroyed many of their best divisions. The Nationalists were poorly led and inefficient, even after seven years of war. The Japanese managed to clear Henan Province and it is certain that this offensive improved the long-term interests of Mao Tse-tung.

◼ *see* Mao Tse-tung p. 223

MAO TSE-TUNG (1893–1976)

In Mao's early years he lived in a country that was going through enormous upheavals. In 1911 the Manchu dynasty fell and for a time Sun Yat-sen came to power, but by 1916 China found itself under military rule. Mao moved to Peking in 1918, where he became involved with Marxists and in 1921 joined the Chinese Communist Party. In 1927 the Kuomitang – Chinese Nationalists – murdered thousands of Communists and so began a bitter civil war. In 1934 Mao became Chairman of the Communist Party and leader of the army. During World War II Mao and Chiang Kai-shek, now leader of the Kuomitang, endured an alliance in order to combat the Japanese, but once they had been defeated, China plunged back into civil war, which ultimately saw Mao's

◀ LEFT: US military leader Joseph Stilwell.

Communists gain control of the country. Mao attempted to steer the country through a series of revolutionary changes until 1969. Mao and China gradually moved in a different direction to their former patron, the Russians, causing an irreparable rift between the two. By 1972, however, Mao, desperately ill, was beginning to take a back seat in politics and leadership. He died in 1976.

see War in China p. 123

OPERATION TUNGSTEN (3 APRIL 1944)

Operation Tungsten was an attempt by the British Royal Navy to destroy or disable theGerman warship *Tirpitz*. The *Tirpitz* was hidden in a Norwegian fjord when she was struck by successive waves of aircraft that had taken off from the carriers HMS *Furious* and HMS *Victorious* on 3 April. The *Tirpitz* was undergoing repairs and was caught completely by surprise. Just as the first strike was taking off, more aircraft left for the target. The *Tirpitz* was hit by at least eight bombs, which kept the vessel out of action for three months. Further attacks were planned, but the original was deemed to be sufficiently successful.

▲ ABOVE: The Tirpitz is destoyed by the Royal Navy.

see Coastal Command p. 225

IMPHALA AND KOHIMA (5 APRIL–22 JUNE 1944)

On 6 March 1944 the Japanese launched their U-Go offensive in northern Burma. It planned to prevent the Allies taking Burma and to break through into India. British offensives had so far failed and the Japanese identified the border town of Imphala, which linked to the hill town of Kohima, as being the most promising line of attack. The Japanese 15th Army moved into Imphala at the same time as Slim was preparing for an offensive, but by 5 April the Japanese had cut the Imphala-Kohima road. Slim knew that it was imperative to deny the mountain roads down to the Indian Plain. Reinforcements were rushed to Kohima. The fighting began when 12,000 Japanese attacked the 1,200-manned garrison of Kohima. By 7 April the situation was desperate; huge Japanese attacks took place between 17 and 18 April, but the Kohima garrison was relieved on 20 April. Fighting continued through May and at the end of the month the Japanese finally withdrew; Imphala itself was relieved on 22 June, after an 80-day siege. Of the 85,000 Japanese who had planned to invade India, only 20,000 were left. The Allies had suffered 17,857 killed, wounded or missing.

�« see War in China p. 123

COASTAL COMMAND (1936–45)

RAF Coastal Command was created on 14 July 1936 and comprised of three groups, one based in Scotland, another in south-east England and the other in western England and the Irish Sea. In total there were 19 squadrons, including six flying-boat squadrons. Their primary role was to patrol the North Sea, German-held coastlines, the northern Atlantic convoy routes and assist in the English Channel defence. They were also charged with making attacks on enemy U-boats and E-boats, performing air-sea rescues, protecting convoys and picking up the crews of sunken ships. Amongst many other vital functions, Coastal Command played a leading role in the evacuation of Dunkirk. It was instrumental in spotting enemy vessels and was involved in the hunting of the Bismarck.

◆ see Sinking of the *Tirpitz* p. 265

NEW GUINEA (22 APRIL–20 AUGUST 1944)

An 84,000-strong task force began landing in New Guinea on 22 April. They would face 11,000 Japanese defenders. The Japanese were heavily bombed prior to the landings and with the exception of protecting the airfields, the majority retreated into the mountains. Throughout late April more US troops landed in New Guinea and reopened an airfield, gaining control of the beachheads. Considerable progress was made in early May and on 16 May a new task force arrived. In the ensuing offensive Japanese casualties reached 9,000. A further invasion fleet arrived on 27 May, but the Japanese garrison, on Biak Island, remained resolutely defiant. The action developed on 29 May, with the first tank battle in the Pacific. Japanese resistance continued until 20 August.

◆ see Saipan p. 237

▶ RIGHT: US paratroopers.

SEVASTOPOL IS LIBERATED (9 MAY 1944)

After enormous resistance in the Crimea, the final pocket of German resistance began to crumble at Sevastopol. The last major thrust by the Russians began on 5 May and within four days the whole of the Crimea was in Russian hands. Small German rearguards held out for a further three days, covering the final German evacuation of the Crimea. In Moscow 24 salvos were fired from 324 guns to celebrate the victory.

T-34 (1939–45)

The T34 was arguably the most important tank of the war. It ensured Russia's survival and Germany's defeat in the east. Initially T34s were encountered in ones or twos, but even so they proved a match for the German tanks. As the Germans advanced they encountered increasing numbers of T34s, which were capable of delivering devastating counterattacks to the German manouevres. Improvements to the T34-76 continued towards the end of 1941, despite the fact that the Germans claimed to have captured or destroyed 20,000 of them. T34s were instrumental in the Russian victory at Kursk (1943). Having achieved this, the Russians moved to produce the T34-85, which became the blueprint for Russian tanks for several decades. This was an up-gunned version of the T34-76, with a different turret and a new five-speed gearbox. It mounted the 85-mm gun which coped with German 75-mm and 88-mm tank and anti-tank guns. The M/39 85-mm anti-aircraft gun had already been developed as a tank gun for use in the KV/85. A new three-man welded or cast turret to house this weapon and mount it on a standard T34 chassis was proposed in an attempt to combat the increasing Panzers.

◆ *see* Soviets Launch Offensive Against Finland p. 236

GERMANS ATTEMPT TO SNATCH TITO (25 MAY 1944)

In their continuing attempt to destroy or subdue Tito's Partisans in Yugoslavia, a crack German paratrooper force was dropped on to Tito's headquarters at Drvar in Bosnia. Tito and Major Randolph Churchill narrowly escaped capture. This was one of the German's last throws of the dice in Yugoslavia, as Russian troops would soon be in a position to link up with Tito's Partisans and push them out of the Balkans.

see Tito Liberates Belgrade and Dubrovnik p. 263

CANARIS IS DISMISSED AS HEAD OF THE ABWEHR (1 JUNE 1944)

For several years Heinrich Himmler had been agitating to gain control of the German army military intelligence unit, the Abwehr, controlled by Admiral Wilhelm Canaris. By insinuation, Himmler had managed to implicate Canaris in plots against Hitler. Indeed, Canaris had been involved in the plots up to 1943, but as a result of his house arrest he was not involved in the July plot of 1944.

see Heinrich Himmler p. 228

HIMMLER, HEINRICH (1900–45)

After working as a fertilizer salesman and chicken farmer, Himmler, a Nazi Party member since the early 1920s, was appointed leader of the Schutzstaffel (SS) in 1929. The SS had less than 300 members at the time, but under

▶ *RIGHT: Nazi Heinrich Himmler.*

Himmler it had swelled to 52,000 by 1933. In June 1934 the rival organization, the Sturm Abteilung, was purged by Himmler and Goering, ensuring his total control of the SS. In 1936, Himmler became leader of the Gestapo and four years later established the Waffen SS, which grew to 150,000 within six months.

Himmler's SS controlled the concentration camps across the occupied lands of Europe and dealt with internal security. By 1944, in the wake of the July plot to assassinate Hitler, Himmler gained control of the Abwehr, with its membership of over 800,000.

Himmler assumed military responsibility on the Western Front and against the Russians in the east (January 1945). Convinced that Germany needed to come to terms with the western Allies or face oblivion, Hitler was informed of Himmler's intentions in April and ordered his arrest. Himmler disappeared, with an assumed name, but was arrested by the British in Bremen on 22 May. He committed suicide before he could be questioned.

◆ see British Capture Himmler p. 296

OPERATION OVERLORD (6 JUNE 1944)

At 09:35 on 6 June 1944 the world was informed that the Allies had finally opened a front in France: 'Under the command of General Eisenhower, Allied naval forces, supported by strong air forces, began landing Allied armies this morning on the northern coast of France.' If anything the statement undersold the enormity of what had been planned. There were 1.7 million fighting troops in Great Britain by June, two million tons of war materials and 50,000 vehicles including tanks. They would be ranged against 500,000 Germans covering 1,287 km (800 miles) of coastline between Brittany and Holland. The blow would fall in Normandy, when a vast armada of 2,727 ships approached five designated beachheads, preceded by a parachute drop involving 20,000 Anglo-American troops and untold numbers of smaller commando and special-forces units striking at key positions in order to seize bridges or eliminate coastal defences. The sheer complexity of the operation beggared belief. The Channel had been turned into a vast, slowly moving stream of vessels, packed with troops and equipment, overflown by an overwhelming number of Allied fighters and bombers. Even as they landed, the Germans were convinced that this was simply a diversionary attack.

AIRBORNE LANDINGS AND RAIDS (6 JUNE 1944)

Landing in advance of the amphibious troops, were the British 6th Airborne and the American 82nd and 101st, totalling some 20,000 men. They dropped inland between St Mère Église and Carentan to support the US landings and to the east of the River Orne to support the Anglo-Canadian landings. Many would fall into swamp area, created by Rommel as an anti-invasion obstacle. The men were scattered far and wide by poor pinpointing of targets, yet 18,000 men succeeded in liberating St Mère Église (the first village in France to be liberated) and to seize control of the Caen Bridge over the River Orne. The Germans were caught entirely unprepared, but they were quickly able to deploy troops to oppose and block the movement of the paratroopers. Nonetheless, it was a chaotic night and the paratrooper landings were often mistaken by the Germans as being diversions, feints, raids or attempts to seize senior German officers. Many of the paratrooper units would, nevertheless, have to hold or seize ground in order to assist their compatriots, driving off the beaches. No German dared wake Hitler, asleep in Berchtesgaden.

◆ see The French Resistance p. 231

THE FRENCH RESISTANCE (1940–45)

The French Resistance was created in the wake of a speech by Charles de Gaulle on 7 June 1940. The Resistance ranged from Socialists and Communists to ex-soldiers or Maquis. Many of the French Resistance were not French at all – they were either Spaniards, foreign nationalists, such as Britons or Americans, or other sundry individuals seeking to keep one pace ahead of the Gestapo. The Resistance used a cell structure in order to minimize their chance of being discovered. Primarily they were involved in helping Allied pilots who had been shot down. Occasionally they would launch attacks on isolated German positions but for the most part they were engaged in intelligence-gathering. From November 1940 the British Special Operations Executive sent in advisors and radio operators, as did the Secret Intelligence Service and the Special Air Service. Charles de

▲ ABOVE: Members of the French Resistance planning an operation.

Gaulle created his own group, the Bureau Central de Renseignements et d'Action (BCRA). The Resistance were constantly hounded by the Gestapo, the Wehrmacht and the Abwehr and, in Vichy France, the notorious Milice. The Resistance received an enormous increase in numbers in 1943 when the Germans initiated a forced labour draft. By that time the US Office of Strategic Services was operating in France.

D-DAY BEACHES (6 JUNE 1944)

The Normandy landings took place along a stretch of the Normandy coast from Quinneville in the west to Ouistreham in the east. The two western beaches were designated as Utah and Omaha and were the concern of Bradley's 1st US Army. The three Anglo-Canadian beaches of Gold, Juno and Sword, were commanded by Dempsey. In overall command of the 21st Army Group was General Montgomery. American progress on their two beaches was comparatively slow and indeed the casualties were higher than expected on both beaches. On the Anglo-

Canadian beaches, however, the troops pushed rapidly inland, heading towards Bayou to the far west of the beaches and towards Caen inland. Unfortunately, the 21st Panzer Division quickly responded and blocked the junction of Juno and Sword beaches. By the end of the

◄ LEFT: Allied troops land on the beaches of Normandy.

first day 155,000 men had landed on French soil. Rommel had always believed that if Germany had any chance of defending mainland Europe, then victory must be achieved on the beaches. In this he had lost the first and most vital battle. The pressure would grow until the break out became irresistible.

➤ see Operation Overlord p. 229

SHERMAN TANK (1939–45)

The Sherman was a remarkable US medium tank which fought in every theatre of the war in the service of every Allied army. The first Shermans were used by the British during El Alamein. Despite criticism about firepower and armour, the Sherman was cheap, easy to produce, rugged, reliable, had low maintenance needs and was fast. Some adaptations included the versions of the M4 with a rocket-projector rack mounted on top of the turret, commonly known as the 'Calliope', mine exploders, flail tanks, mine excavators, bulldozers, hedge-cutters and flamethrowers, as well as rocket launchers. These adaptations of

▼ BELOW: A US Sherman tank.

the Sherman, from the M4 through to the M4A6, ceased production in June 1945, but the US army still used the Sherman in large numbers during the Korean War.

STUBBORN GERMAN RESISTANCE (6–27 JUNE 1944)

By 8 June 1944, in the face of growing German resistance, the British had managed to link up with the American beaches. The Germans still held Carentan, but pressure from the 101st Airborne cleared the town on 11 July. The Germans began counterattacking around Caen, halting the British drive on the town. By 12 June the US troops on Utah had still not reached the line of occupation they had meant to seize on the first day, yet assistance was on its way from Omaha beach. The British were able to punch through to Villers-Bocage by 13 June, whilst US troops attempted to cut off Cherbourg. Fighting was particularly intense around Caen and would remain so for a considerable time.

see Cherbourg Falls p. 239

OPERATION NEPTUNE (6 JUNE–2 JULY 1944)

Operation Neptune was the codename for the logistical movement of men and materials across the English Channel to the Normandy beaches. It was a vast undertaking and required a precision and coordination the like of which had never been attempted before. By 12 June some 326,000 men, 104,000 tons of war materials and 54,000 vehicles had made the Channel crossing. By 2 July this had leapt to 929,000 men, 586,000 tons of equipment and 177,000 vehicles. This was the crucial phase of the operation. Operation Neptune did not end with the break out from the beaches and the pursuit of the Germans across France; by 15 August 1944 over two million men had crossed the Channel.

see D-Day Beaches p. 232

MULBERRY HARBOURS (1944)

One of the major problems choosing Normandy as the site for the invasion was the lack of immediate harbour facilities to bring in troops and equipment. The problem was solved in the most remarkable of ways. Vast floating concrete blocks, 60 m (197 ft) long, 18 m (59 ft) high and 15 m (49 ft) wide, were joined together to create two separate harbours, some 9.5 km (6 miles) in length. Further out to sea, nearly 60 obsolete merchant ships were sunk to form a breakwater. Remarkably, despite poor weather conditions, the Mulberry Harbours continued to be invaluable far beyond their intended period of use. The original design was by Professor Bernal who proposed it in 1943. The designs were developed by Brigadier Bruce White who created the final look for the Mulberry Harbours.

◆ see Cherbourg Falls p. 239

▲ ABOVE: A Mulberry Harbours, used in the D-Day landings.

SOVIETS LAUNCH AN OFFENSIVE AGAINST FINLAND (8 JUNE 1944)

By 8 June 1944 the Russians and the Finns had still been unable to reach an agreement regarding disputed territories and alliances. Therefore, after a three-hour artillery bombardment, two Russian armies were pitted against the Finnish defence lines between Lake Ladoga and the Gulf of Finland to decide the matter once and for all. A truce was finally agreed on 19 September. The sticking point would remain Russia's reluctance to accept Finland's sovereignty.

◆ *see* Finns and Soviets Agree a Ceasefire p. 252

ORADOUR-SUR-GLANE MASSACRE (10 JUNE 1944)

On 10 June 1944 groups from the SS Das Reich Division began rounding up the 652 inhabitants of Oradour-Sur-Glase. They were told that they were suspected of hiding explosives and that the village would be systematically checked. The men were locked up in barns and the women and children in the church. The German troops then set fire to the village and shot anyone who tried to escape. Only 10 people survived the massacre.

◆ *see* Soviets Liberate the First Concentration Camp p. 245

B-29s CARRY OUT FIRST RAID ON JAPAN (15 JUNE 1944)

Having established relatively firm bases on mainland China, the US started to plan a periodic bombing campaign on mainland Japan. The US 20th Bomber Command had established several B-29 Super Fortress airfields and on 15 June 1944 carried out their first bombing raid on Japan. Their target was a steelworks factory at Jawata on Kyushu Island. In this first raid they managed to drop 200 bombs on target.

◆ *see* Tokyo Firebomb Raid p. 279

▲ *ABOVE: US battleships attack the Japanese at Saipan.*

SAIPAN (15 JUNE 1944)

At 05:45 on 15 June an enormous bombardment preceded the arrival of 700 landing craft, carrying elements of two US marine divisions on the west coast of Saipan. They faced 30,000 Japanese troops but managed to secure a beachhead 8.9 km (5.5 miles) wide and 1.2 km (0.75 miles) deep by the end of the first day. The Japanese launched a series of suicidal attacks during the night but were unable to dislodge the marines who were now firmly dug in. The Japanese continued to resist throughout June but by the end of the month their resistance in the south had ended. The island did not fall until 9 July, by which time 30,000 Japanese had died to the Americans 14,000.

THE MARIANAS TURKEY SHOOT (19 JUNE 1944)

Officially, at least, this engagement should be known as the Battle of the Philippine Sea: aircraft from nine Japanese aircraft carriers engaged those from 15 US aircraft carriers in the skies above the Marianas. The Japanese were also supported by aircraft from their nearby land bases. In near-suicidal attacks against the American fleet, the Japanese lost 400 aircraft in just one day, claiming 130 American planes. Battle continued into the next day, but, bereft of air cover, three Japanese aircraft carriers were obliterated, along with two destroyers and a fuel tanker. Ozawa, the Japanese commander, prudently decided to retire. The engagement is known as the Marianas turkey shoot due to the inexperience of the Japanese pilots.

◆ see The Divine Wind p. 238

THE DIVINE WIND (1944)

By 1944 the war had turned against Japan. Vice Admiral Takijiro Ohnishi, commander of the First Air Fleet, proposed setting up suicide units. The first was formed at Mabalacat airbase in the Philippines and included 26 pilots of the 201st Air Group, First Air Fleet of the Imperial Japanese Naval Air Force who joined the Kamikaze (Divine Wind) unit. Several such units were created and on 20 October the first 26 aircraft lifted off from Cebu airbase seeking out US vessels. They failed to find their targets at first but finally struck at Leyte Gulf, crashing into the aircraft carriers USS *Santee* and *Suwanee*. Other members of the group attacked the USS *Kitkun Bay* and the *St Lô*, the latter being sunk. Kamikaze missions became an integral part of Japanese Air Force strategy. The suicide bombers were escorted by fighter aircraft to ensure they reached their targets. A new recruit had two week's flight training and a 10-day attack course; the best pilots retained as escorts.

◆ see US Captures Saipan p. 243

OPERATION BAGRATION (23 JUNE 1944)

In the summer of 1944 the Russians mustered 166 divisions to attack at six points in Belorussia; their final objective was the city of Minsk. They would face 38 depleted German divisions. Pivotal in this offensive was the Moscow–Minsk road and the Smolensk–Minsk railroad. Despite the fact that German intelligence had received notice of the attack, their defences were simply too weak to resist.

see Soviets Liberate Minsk p. 241

CHERBOURG FALLS (27 JUNE 1944)

By 20 June 1944 the pressure on Cherbourg was becoming intense and the following day the Germans were asked to surrender. No reply was received. On 22 June, after an intense bombardment, the US launched their assault. Many German units instantly surrendered and by the following day the Allies were able to penetrate the outer defences. Fighting continued through 24 June and it became clear that it would only take one more push to gain control of the town. The German commander asked Rommel for permission to surrender. He replied 'in accordance with the Führer's orders, you are to hold out to the last round'. Cherbourg surrendered on 27 June.

see Breakthrough at Caen p. 241

▶ *RIGHT: US troops enter Cherbourg.*

GOEBBELS, JOSEPH (1897–1945)

Goebbels was the intellectual of the Nazi Party. At first he was opposed to Hitler, but by 1926 he had shifted allegiance and was masterminding the propaganda, street fights and parades that characterized the party's strategy. In 1929 Hitler promoted him to Reich Propaganda Leader and Goebbels is credited with moulding Hitler into an effective speaker, creating the cult around the Führer and demonizing the Jews and the Communists.

It was Goebbels who helped sweep the Nazis to power in 1932. Hitler appointed him Reich Minister for Public Enlightenment and Propaganda, giving him complete control of the media. Before the war, Goebbels masterminded the book-burnings in 1933 and Kristallnacht in 1938. Geobbels was a strong supporter of the 'Final Solution' and directed the deportation of Berlin's Jewish population in 1942. Goebbels saved Hitler and the Nazi regime in the aftermath of the July 1944 attempt to assassinate Hitler by rounding up the conspirators. To the end, he remained Hitler's most loyal follower, choosing death for himself, his wife and six children in the Berlin bunker on 1 May 1945, despite having been named Reich Chancellor by Hitler in his last order.

see July Plot p. 244

▲ ABOVE: Joseph Goebbels reviewing his troops in Berlin.

SOVIETS LIBERATE MINSK (3 JULY 1944)

As the Russians marched into Minsk, the German Army Group Centre found 28 of its 40 divisions encircled. As a result of the fighting in the area, some 400,000 Germans had been killed, 158,000 taken prisoner, 2,000 tanks and 10,000 guns captured. What remained of the German front was now completely exposed. The Soviets had no difficulty in restoring liberty to the city.

◆ *see* Warsaw Resistance Army Rises p. 247

BREAKTHROUGH AT CAEN (8 JULY 1944)

After many delays and false starts, at 04:20 on 8 July 1944, British I Corps launched its offensive against Caen, throwing three divisions against the city. The suburbs had been breached on 9 July, with the Canadian 3rd Division coming in from the west and the British 1st Division from the north. The 12th SS Panzer Division could do little to stop them. The following day a major offensive was opened south-west of Caen and by 11 July they had pushed 21 km (13 miles) to the west of the city. By 18 July the whole of the Canadian II Corps had crossed the Orne River and captured Colombelles and Giberville. The British VII Corps was engaged in a desperate struggle against the 1st SS Panzer Group to the south of Caen.

THE FIGHTING SS (1940–45)

The Waffen SS, or armed SS units, were created in 1940 and in most respects they can be differentiated from the SS-Totenkopfverbande ('death's head') units as they were primarily an elite military formation. By the end of the war some 600,000 men were serving in the Waffen SS, the fourth branch of the German Wehrmacht, although its control still remained within the hands of the SS. Waffen SS units would spearhead some of the most important battles of the war and were often given the most difficult combat challenges. They are, however, closely associated with innumerable war crimes, largely as a result of the political instructions and indoctrination given to them, rather than their prowess in battle. Waffen SS units invariably received the latest German equipment and were first in line for supplies, replacements and honours. Theoretically, there were 38 Waffen SS divisions, including the Leibstandarte Adolf Hitler, Das Reich, Totenkopf, Wiking and Hitlerjugend. Waffen SS units were primarily used for offensives but as the situation grew more critical they were increasingly deployed in a defensive role, rotated backwards and forwards between the east and western fronts.

◼ see Operation Cobra p. 245

▼ BELOW: German SS troops.

▲ ABOVE: US marines during the capture of Saipan.

US CAPTURE SAIPAN (9 JULY 1944)

After ruinous combat since the middle of June, US troops finally reached Point Marpi on Saipan – the objective of their offensive – on 9 July. Only a handful at the Japanese garrison had been taken prisoner and at Point Marpi the marines discovered the grisly atrocity left by the Japanese. They had systematically thrown hundreds of civilians over the cliffs to their doom.

◪ see Guam p. 244

TOJO IS RELIEVED OF HIS COMMAND (18 JULY 1944)

The loss of Saipan was the final straw for the Japanese government. They had relied on Tojo to guide the country to victory, but on 18 July he was relieved as Chief of General Staff and replaced by General Yoshijiro Umezu. The following day the Japanese government resigned and Emperor Hirohito asked General Koiso to form a new government.

◆ see Hideki Tojo p. 121

JULY PLOT (20 JULY 1944)

An elaborate anti-Nazi plot sprang into action on 20 July 1944. The plan involved the murder of Hitler, Goering and Himmler. Von Stauffenberg placed a bomb in Hitler's conference room, which succeeded in killing four people, but only injuring Hitler. Other conspirators would seize Berlin and eliminate Goering and Himmler. Hitler survived and the plotters were rounded up, tortured and slowly executed. Around 4,980 Germans were executed as a result of the plot.

◆ see Adolf Hitler p. 54

GUAM (21 JULY–10 AUGUST 1944)

After a massive air and naval bombardment, the 3rd Marine Division and elements of the 77th Infantry Division began landing on the west coast of Guam in the Marianas at 08:30 on 21 July. They were quickly able to establish a beachhead 3 km (2 miles) wide and 1.6 km (1 mile) deep. They faced 12,000 Japanese under Takashima's command. On 25 July the Japanese launched seven attacks and lost 3,500 men. By 28 July Takashima was dead and US marines had reached the edge of the airfield. By 1 August half the island was in US hands and Japanese resistance ended on 10 August, having suffered at least 15,000 casualties. US forces, despite overwhelming firepower, had suffered 1,400 casualties.

◆ see US Land at Leyte p. 263

SOVIETS LIBERATE THE FIRST CONCENTRATION CAMP (24 JULY 1944)

Russian troops discovered what was left of the Majdanek concentration camp on 24 July 1944. The camp had been in operation since February 1943 and around 130,000 Jews had been slaughtered there, in addition to Polish prisoners and Soviet prisoners of war. It has been estimated that around 200,000 people perished in this camp altogether. Several thousand inmates were still alive amongst the dead when the camp was liberated.

◇ *see* Jews and Ethnic Minorities in Occupied Europe p. 246

OPERATION COBRA (25 JULY 1944)

The much-awaited breakout from the beaches of Normandy was achieved by the sheer weight of German troops being attracted into the Caen area to deal with the British and Canadians forces in action there. This left the American 1st Army with the comparatively simple task of punching through towards St Lô. Codenamed Operation Cobra, a complete breakthrough was made between 25 and 27 July. By the following day, US troops were advancing southwards on the west bank of the River Vire to the east of St Lô.

On 30 July the Germans launched a massive counterattack, which temporarily held off the advancing Americans. On the first day of August General Patton assumed command of the US 3rd Army and was given the job of holding the extreme right of the Allied line. On 5 August his units approached Brest and St Malo, while other units were pushing deep into Brittany. Elements of Patton's army reached the outskirts of Brest in the evening of 7 August and the following day the Germans were asked to surrender. The request was met with a point-blank refusal.

◇ *see* Patton's Corps p. 246

PATTON'S CORPS (1943–45)

George Patton was an archetypal cavalry commander, born perhaps 100 years after his time. Nonetheless, he swiftly adapted to the concept of commanding tracked vehicles and fast-moving columns of troops in numerous campaigns from 1943. His corps had been involved in the original Torch landings in 1943 and had shown considerable dash in their race across Sicily in order to beat Montgomery to Messina. When Operation Overlord was launched, Patton's troops were not landed in France until August but were then placed exactly where Patton could do the most damage. With the British holding the Germans down at Caen, it wasn't long before he found the roads of France open and swept virtually unopposed through the countryside, helping to hasten the defeat of the Axis powers in the west.

◧ see The Falaise Gap p. 249

▶ RIGHT: General George Patton.

JEWS AND ETHNIC MINORITIES IN OCCUPIED EUROPE (1940–45)

The Germans used a variety of different legislation and propaganda in order to consign the Jewish population of Europe and other 'undesirable ethnic groups' into ghettos, prior to 'resettling' them (a euphemism for deportation to concentration or death camps). The Nuremberg laws issued in 1935 meant that only Germans – and by that the Nazis meant Aryans – had a right to be citizens within the Reich. As the size and influence of the Reich and its territories grew, wherever Jews or ethnic minorities lived, they were brought under the dictates of the law. Jews were not the only ones persecuted, though: Political adversaries, common criminals, prisoners of war from countries the Nazis considered inferior and gypsies, all came in for harsh treatment and eventual liquidation by the Nazis. Forced labour was another issue which impacted upon the Jews in particular. Workshops were set up in special labour camps or in ghettos where men, women and children would be worked to death. Step by step the Nazi policy was to identify, degrade and then eliminate all undesirables within their reach.

◆ *see* Arrest of Anne Frank and Her Family p. 248

WARSAW RESISTANCE ARMY RISES (1 AUGUST 1944)

In eager anticipation of the imminent arrival of Russian troops, Polish patriots staged an uprising in Warsaw, hoping their presence would ensure an independent post-war Poland. For political reasons, Russian troops advancing on the city paused in the suburb of Praga on the opposite side of the Vistula River. They waited until the Polish resistance army had been surrounded and wiped out by the Germans before they continued their advance.

▶ RIGHT: *Women of the Warsaw Resistance.*

SOVIETS REACH BALTIC SEA (4 AUGUST 1944)

Facing increasing pressure, the German Army Group North temporarily managed to hold off Russian attempts to capture Riga. On 1 August the Russians had captured Kaunas, the capital of Lithuania. The German attack reopened the Estonian-Latvian corridor between Riga and the Russian salient at Jelgava, the end of a 724-km (450-mile) supply line.

ARREST OF ANNE FRANK AND HER FAMILY (4 AUGUST 1944)

Anne Frank was born on 12 June 1930. After the Nazi invasion of Holland, she and her family and four other Jews sought refuge in a few rooms above her father's office in Amsterdam, in an effort to avoid being deported to one of the many concentration camps that had been built as labour or extermination camps. They were under constant threat of discovery but she was betrayed in August 1944 after spending 25 months in hiding. She was arrested and deported to a concentration camp. She died in Bergen-Belsen in March 1945 at the age of 15. Her diary, which she kept during her period of hiding, described her everyday life and her fears. Her diary, which survived the war, has been translated into 55 different languages.

OPERATION DRAGOON-ANVIL (15 AUGUST 1944)

Operation Dragoon-Anvil was the codename for the Allied landings on the south coast of France, involving 2,000 transport and landing craft, escorted by 300 warships. In one day, 94,000 men were landed and established a solid beachhead. A German attack ended in failure with the loss of 15,000 men and 4,000 vehicles. By the end of August some 48,000 prisoners had fallen into Allied hands.

◆ see Operation Overlord p. 229

FALAISE GAP (16–20 AUGUST 1944)

On 16 August 1944 Canadian troops entered Falaise, whilst the British I Corps moved towards the River Seine. To the south US forces had reached Dreux and Chartres. Almost trapped around Falaise were the German 5th Armoured Army and the 7th Army, amounting to some 250,000 Germans. The Falaise Gap was sealed on 20 August and within the pocket a fearful slaughter began, with Allied aircraft ranging at will across the battlefield, destroying any German tank or vehicle that came into sight. The German troops who had been defending German-held France for so long were now trapped and the Allies showed little mercy until every formation and unit was ready to

▲ ABOVE: The bomb-wrecked city of Falaise, as it was found by the Canadian troops in 1944.

offer unconditional surrender. Their loss hastened the end in the west and with it the fall of Paris. The Allied forces were now advancing towards the borders of Germany itself. German losses included 200,000 prisoners and at least 50,000 deaths. Some 240,000 men had managed to break through at various points, but these reached the safety of the German lines with little more than the clothes on their backs.

TYPHOON TANK BUSTER (1941–45)

It was canon fire from a Hawker Typhoon fighter bomber of 266 Squadron that effectively took Field Marshall Rommel out of the war, when it swooped on his staff car in Normandy in 1944. Rommel was so seriously injured that he played no further part in command operations. The Typhoon had its maiden flight on 26 May 1941 and it came into service the following September. The Typhoon had originally been thought of as a successor to the Hurricane, but it was in its ground-attack role, particularly after D-Day, that it came into its own. The RAF had 26 squadrons of these aircraft, which had a maximum speed of 641 kph (398 mph). During the Battle of Normandy the Typhoons accounted for 137 tanks around Avranches. In total 3,330 Typhoons were built.

◆ see Liberation of Paris p. 250

LIBERATION OF PARIS (15 AUGUST 1944)

On 19 August an uprising arose in Paris against the German occupation. There was bitter street fighting, but already the French 2nd Armoured Division was moving towards Paris and on 23 August the US 4th Division entered Arpajon, to the south of the city. By 24 August Leclerc was close to the south-western

◀ LEFT: Civilians and troops celebrating the liberation of Paris.

suburbs of Paris and running into some difficulties. The US 4th Division was ordered to attack from the south and two bridgeheads were secured over the River Seine. At 07:00 on 25 August Leclerc's troops entered Paris from the south-west and half an hour later the US 4th Division broke through in the south. The German commander, in defiance of Hitler's orders to raze Paris, surrendered the city. Liberation officially occurred at 15:15. The following day the Canadians headed towards Calais, while the British thrust towards Belgium and the US 1st Army began moving along the Paris–Brussels Road. German troops were still holding out in Brittany and Brest still defied the Allies. On 28 August Leclerc continued his advance north-east and Allied troops aimed to cross the River Somme.

◆ *see* Liberation of Brussels p. 251

▲ *ABOVE: Troops being welcomed by citizens of Liège.*

LIBERATION OF BRUSSELS (3 SEPTEMBER 1944)

The provisional French government transferred back to Paris on 31 August, while Allied troops established a bridgehead over the River Meuse, near Verdun. On 1 September Verdun was liberated and the Canadians reached Dieppe. Advances were already being made towards Metz. On 2 September the US 1st Army had almost reached the Belgian frontier, while the British advanced towards Le Havre. The following day

Brussels itself was liberated by XXX Corps. The next day the British unit took Antwerp. On 5 September the Allies enjoyed a series of successes: Boulogne was taken; the Meuse was crossed at Sedan; and the Moselle near Nancy. The following day Liege was also liberated and the outskirts of Bruges were reached on 8 September.

🔹 *see* German and Dutch Borders are Crossed p. 253

FINNS AND SOVIETS AGREE A CEASEFIRE (4 SEPTEMBER 1944)

On 2 September the new Finnish Prime Minister, Antti Hackzell broke off diplomatic relations with Germany. Two days later the Finns requested a ceasefire and an armistice was agreed between the Finnish and the Russian governments. On 6 September the Finnish delegation arrived in Moscow to discuss the armistice.

🔹 *see* Soviets Declare War on Bulgaria p. 252

SOVIETS DECLARE WAR ON BULGARIA (5 SEPTEMBER 1944)

On 5 September the Russians declared war on Bulgaria and sent their troops across the border within hours of the declaration. They had barely got underway when Bulgaria surrendered. On 7 September Bulgaria declared war on Germany and they agreed to allow occupation by Russian troops. Four Russian armies, one motorized corps and one air army entered Bulgaria to take over the occupation.

🔹 *see* Soviets Push into Prussia p. 262

V2 ROCKET HITS LONDON (8 SEPTEMBER 1944)

The V2 rocket, or Vergeltungswaffe ('reprisal weapon 2'), was a vast early attempt at an intercontinental missile. In truth it had a limited range, and had been built at the slave-labour camp of Dora, near Nordhausen in Germany. The first battery to reach operational stage had intended to fire

▲ ABOVE: Bomb damage on a London street.

on Paris, but after several launch failures, rockets were fired from the vicinity of Houffalize and The Hague on London.

◆ see German Rocket Programme p. 271

GERMAN AND DUTCH BORDERS ARE CROSSED (9 SEPTEMBER 1944)

The US XIX Corps reached the Maastricht area on 9 September, crossing the borders of Belgium and Holland. The push towards Antwerp was postponed due to the imminent Operation Market Garden. By 11 September the entire French Channel coast, with the exception of Boulogne, Calais and Dunkirk, was in Allied hands. On the same day, units of the US 1st Army crossed the German border near Aachen, creating panic amongst the locals.

◆ see Operation Market Garden p. 254

OPERATION MARKET GARDEN (17 SEPTEMBER 1944)

Operation Market Garden was launched on Sunday 17 September and involved the dropping of a carpet of paratroopers throughout Holland to the Rhine. The plan had been conceived by General Montgomery, against stiff opposition from Patton and Eisenhower. The British 1st Airborne Army would be dropped in and around Arnhem, with the task of capturing the bridges over the lower Rhine. The US 101st would land to the north of Eindhoven and the 82nd would land near Grave to the south of Nijmegen. They would hold the vital bridges until such a time as Horrock's XXX Corps could push up through the corridor and reach Arnhem. The British paratroopers found powerful German forces on the ground around Arnhem and only a portion of the force managed to break through to the Arnhem Bridge. The 101st managed to take its objectives and held the bridges over the Wilhelmina and Zuiter Willemsvaart Canals. The 82nd, meanwhile, managed to capture the bridge at Grave, but were denied the Nijmegen Bridge due to heavy German opposition. XXX Corps managed to join up with the 101st to the north of Eindhoven on 18 September, but German troops were being rushed in increasing numbers to the area.

◆ see Red Devils p. 254

RED DEVILS (1942–45)

Although late in creating airborne troops, the British had in their paratroopers some of the finest soldiers, capable of carrying out missions from small raids to enormous operations. One of their first tests came on 28 February 1942, when 120 men, led by Major John Frost, dropped over Bruneval radar station in occupied France. Sterner testing occurred in November 1942, when they dropped to seize the enemy airfield at Oudna in Tunisia. Whilst they were deployed in advance of amphibious landings in Normandy, it is Operation Market Garden that established their immortality. Three divisions landed along a narrow stretch of Dutch countryside to secure the bridges which the British XXX Corps needed to drive to Arnhem. Following intense fighting the paratroopers fulfilled all obligations except taking the southern end of Arnhem Bridge.

see Operation Market Garden p. 254

THE ARNHEM LANDINGS (17 SEPTEMBER 1944)

The British paratroopers who had managed to reach the Arnhem Bridge were cut off and German troops were massing all around the British perimeter. By 19 September it was obvious that the rest of the paratroopers could not break through to Arnhem. On 21 September the paratroopers dug in on the north bank of the Rhine to the west of Oosterbeek, determined to hold out until XXX Corps reached them. By now those at the Arnhem Bridge had been overwhelmed. In desperation, Polish paratroopers were dropped to the south of the Rhine and Eindhoven, but they could not cross the river to link up with the British paratroopers. On 26 September, 2,200 of the original 10,000 men managed to re-cross the Rhine to safety.

US AIRBORNE FORCES (1942–45)

The 82nd Airborne was the first US airborne unit. It was earmarked to spearhead the landings for Operation Husky and its objective would be to seize and hold the high ground above the beaches in Sicily that would be used by Patton's Divisions. As it turned out the 82nd would find themselves scattered across 105 km (65 miles) of coastline. They were closely engaged by the Herman Goering Panzer Division but they held off the enemy counterattacks until they saw the welcome sight of Sherman tanks. The 82nd was then used for the Salerno landings in September

1943 and again for Operation Overlord in June 1944. The 101st Airborne, known as the Screaming Eagles, were created in August 1942. They first saw action during Operation Overlord and were an integral part of Operation Market Garden. Their finest hour, however, occurred over Christmas 1944, when they held Bastogne against German attempts to seize the crossroads to Antwerp. Elements of the division were surrounded on 21 December, but they refused to surrender, forcing the Germans to bypass them. The Germans launched their last assault before dawn on Christmas Day, but elements of the 4th Armoured Division came to their timely rescue.

NIJMEGEN (17–25 SEPTEMBER 1944)

The seizing of the bridges at Grave and Nijmegen were the responsibility of the 82nd Airborne. Paratroopers were dropped either side of the Grave Bridge, but at Nijmegen this did not happen as it was considered that the Groesbeek Heights, a plateau some 91 m (300 ft) above the bridge, was more important. The priority became to capture the heights before an attempt was made on the bridge itself. As a result, the Nijmegen Highway Bridge was not taken, allowing the Germans to send troops across to hold back XXX Corps. The bridge was finally taken in a breathtaking attack by troops in assault groups across the Waal River. The paratroopers lost half of their force, but 200 of them established a bridgehead, allowing the capture of the bridge.

see Operation Market Garden p. 254

EINDHOVEN (17–25 SEPTEMBER 1944)

Initially the 101st met with little resistance and captured the bridge at Veghel. Significantly, however, German anti-tank guns held off the 101st long enough for the Son Bridge to be destroyed. The 101st had only one

▲ ABOVE: Allied tanks crossing the Nijmegen bridge.

other option – to capture the bridge at Best – but they could not break through. Efforts were then concentrated on moving south to reach the northern end of Eindhoven. By noon they had linked up with advanced units from XXX Corps. At 16:00 they made radio contact and requested that a Bailey Bridge be brought forward. By the evening XXX Corps were in Eindhoven, camped to the south of the wreckage of the Son Bridge while they awaited the arrival of the Royal Engineers to build the bridge. On 19 September the Germans made a determined attack to destroy the Bailey Bridge before it had been built. They were beaten back by increasing numbers of XXX Corps. By the time XXX Corps were in a position to cross, the Germans had positioned heavy units on either side of the road, making an advance towards Arnhem suicidal. By 23 September XXX Corps were a few kilometres from Arnhem, but another German force moved to block the road.

🔄 see XXX Corps p. 258

XXX CORPS (1944)

Horrocks's XXX Corps faced the tremendous task of getting 30,000 vehicles along one road to Arnhem in just three days. Each hold-up blocked the road and each brought the chances of success further from their grasp. XXX Corps had fought as a unit in North Africa, Sicily and mainland Italy, before being transferred back to Britain in preparation for Operation Overlord. They had fought on the beaches in Normandy and then across France into Belgium and were now poised on Dutch soil waiting to thrust the dagger into Germany's heart. Although three parachute divisions had been dropped along the corridor and massive artillery and air bombardment had taken place either side of the road, there were still considerable numbers of hidden German units ready to ambush the column. The most difficult situation occurred at Eindhoven, where one of the vital bridges had been destroyed. It took 36 hours to construct the Bailey Bridges. XXX Corps were ultimately blamed for not pressing forward with the required speed, but even when failure was imminent, Horrocks was still determined to press on and reach Arnhem.

see Brian Horrocks p. 258

HORROCKS, BRIAN (1895–1985)

Horrocks was a career soldier, commissioned into the army in 1914. On 21 October that year, he was wounded and captured by the Germans on the Western Front. He also fought

◀ LEFT: Brian Horrocks.

as a volunteer in the Russian Civil War, being captured once again, this time by the Red Army; he was released in 1920.

By 1939 Horrocks was in France with Montgomery and during the Dunkirk evacuation he became a Brigadier. After Dunkirk, he took command of defences in the Brighton area in anticipation of the German invasion. When Montgomery took over from Auchinleck in North Africa in August 1942, Horrocks joined him, fighting all the way to Tunisia in 1943. Horrocks had been badly wounded in an aircraft attack in June 1943, but was to return to active service by mid-1944. Horrocks commanded XXX Corps for the D-Day landings and for Operation Market Garden. He commanded the troops who successfully captured Amiens, Brussels, Antwerp and Bremen between June 1944 and April 1945. After the end of hostilities Horrocks returned to Britain and worked for the BBC. He died in 1985.

THE POLISH LANDINGS (21 SEPTEMBER 1944)

At 17:00 on 21 September, 1,000 Polish paratroopers dropped to the south of the Rhine. A further 500 had been held up in Britain due to poor weather conditions. The Poles made straight for a ferry across the Rhine, intending to relieve the British airborne troops. Unfortunately the ferry had been destroyed. The Poles, under Sosabowski, tried everything they could to secure a crossing of the Rhine, but each attempt met with failure. They were, however, on hand to cover the evacuation of the exhausted British troops when they could finally leave. On 22 September they attempted a last crossing of the river by attaching boats to a signal cable. It was unfortunately spotted by the Germans and only 52 Poles had managed to cross.

◄► see A Bridge Too Far p. 260

A BRIDGE TOO FAR (25 SEPTEMBER 1944)

Operation Market Garden was undoubtedly one of the most audacious plans proposed during the war. It required that all the bridges needed to convey XXX Corps to Arnhem and across the Rhine should be seized and held against German opposition. Indeed, Allied intelligence had ignored the fact that there were units in the Arnhem area in particular, which had not been anticipated. The RAF had refused to drop the British paratroopers close to the target bridge because this would place them too close to flak guns. Drop zones south of the bridge were also rejected because they were unsuitable for gliders. Instead the British airborne units were dropped 15 km (9 miles) away from the bridge; they therefore needed fast-moving vehicles to seize the bridge while they still had the element of surprise. In Montgomery's own words, Market Garden was 90 per cent successful, he said: 'In my prejudiced view, if the operation had been properly backed from its inception, and given the aircraft, ground forces, and administrative resources necessary for the job, it would have succeeded in spite of my mistakes, or the adverse weather conditions, or the presence of the 22nd SS Panzer Corps in the Arnhem area.'

🔄 *see* Battle of Aachen p. 261

ME262 (1942–45)

The Me262 was a revolutionary turbojet engine aircraft, originally designed by Messerschmitt in 1938. It first flew on 18 July 1942, but the Luftwaffe was cautious and there were developmental problems with it. By late 1943, Hitler had insisted that the aircraft be introduced as a fighter-bomber, but it was not until 25 July 1944 that the first Me262 was used in combat, when one attacked a British aircraft over Munich. The Me262 was deadly as a fighter/interceptor against the vast streams of Allied bombers over Germany, but in fact, of the 1,400 built, only around 300 saw combat.

By this stage the German Luftwaffe was lacking spares, trained pilots and sufficient fuel to commit large numbers to the air. The aircraft was powered by twin Junkers turbojets and had a maximum speed of 870 kph (541 mph). Its practical ceiling was 11,500 m (37,730 ft) and it had a range of just 480 km (298 miles). The heavy armoured aircraft was fitted with four canons and 24 unguided rockets on the wings. This gave the aircraft an operational weight of some 6,396 kg.

◆ *see* Operation Bodenplatte p. 274

BATTLE OF AACHEN (1–21 OCTOBER 1944)

On 1 October 1944 the US 1st Army began its operations aimed at surrounding Aachen. After an artillery and air bombardment, US forces began advancing between Aachen and Geilenkirchen on 2 October. By the next day they had penetrated the Siegfried Line and had been caught up by the 2nd Armoured Division. On 4 October the Germans launched a counter-attack to close the gap, but by now the American V Corps was preparing to enter the action. On 5 October the road to Aachen was cut off and vicious German counterattacks took place around

◀ *LEFT: Wreckage surrounding the cathedral at Aachen after the battle.*

Metz. On 10 October the US 1st Division delivered an ultimatum to German troops in Aachen, ordering them to surrender. The ultimatum expired unanswered the following day and the assault was resumed. The bombing and shelling continued into 12 October and on the 13th the Americans prepared for their final assault. Street fighting continued for a number of days but by 20 October the Germans only held the southern suburbs. Finally, at 12:05 on 21 October, after the city had been reduced to rubble, the German garrison surrendered.

see Hitler's Last Gamble p. 267

ATHENS IS LIBERATED (15 OCTOBER 1944)

On 14 October 1944 the British 3rd Corps and a number of Greek units were poised to land at Piraeus. Their landing was temporarily held up by mines in the harbour. On the previous day British Commandos and Greek troops had landed near Piraeus and occupied the Kalamata airfield. British troops entered Athens on 15 October, determined to deal with the Greek insurrectionists who were already in control of the city.

see Tito Liberates Belgrade and Dubrovnik p. 263

SOVIETS PUSH INTO PRUSSIA (18 OCTOBER 1944)

The major Russian offensive against East Prussia – begun on 18 October – was met by strong German resistance, but the Russians had already penetrated Czechoslovakia and on 20 October the Germans were driven out of Debrecen in Hungary. On 21 October the Russians reached the River Danube and the following day they managed to break through the defences in East Prussia but were halted at Insterburg. For the rest of the year the front in this sector would remain unchanged. Operations were continuing in Romania, however, and the Russians had now occupied

Transylvania. In Hungary, by 26 October, the front had stabilized along the River Tisza. By 1 November Russian troops were close to Budapest.

◐ *see* Soviets Reach Budapest p. 270

TITO LIBERATES BELGRADE AND DUBROVNIK (20 OCTOBER 1944)

On 16 October vicious fighting broke out in Belgrade between Tito's partisans and the Germans. To the south the Russians had occupied Nish. By 18 October Belgrade was on the point of falling into partisan and Russian hands as Army Group F began to retreat from the Balkans. On 20 October Belgrade was liberated and Tito's partisans managed to capture Dubrovnik.

US LAND AT LEYTE (20 OCTOBER 1944)

At 10:05 on 20 October, the lead units of some 120,000 men began landing on the east coast of Leyte Island in the Philippines. MacArthur himself was in overall command. He reminded the Filipinos of his promise to return. The invasion force would face 260,000 Japanese deployed across the islands. On 21 October Japanese suicide attacks were beaten off and the following day US troops moved inland.

◐ *see* Battle of Leyte Gulf p. 263

BATTLE OF LEYTE GULF (23–25 OCTOBER 1944)

From the outset of this bitter battle, there were huge casualties to both the US and Japanese fleets. At 05:32 on 23 October the *Atago* became the first casualty, swiftly followed by the *Maya* at 05:54, both victims of US submarines. At 08:30 on 24 October the USS *Princeton* was hit by enemy aircraft and was finished off by her own ships that afternoon. Between 10:27 and 19:35 the Japanese battleship *Musashy* was hit by several torpedoes and eventually sank. The battle was rejoined the following day

▲ *ABOVE: Troops on the beach at the Battle of Leyte Gulf.*

with opposing destroyer flotillas engaging. The Japanese battleship *Fuso* was sunk at 04:18 and later in the day, after both sides had suffered destroyer losses, the Japanese heavy cruiser *Suzuya* sank at 13:22. Once again the fleets locked horns on 25 October; there were more destroyer losses but the Americans had found three Japanese aircraft carriers. At 09:37 the aircraft carrier *Chitose* was hit and sunk; 14:14 the *Zuikaku* capsized, joined at 15:26 by the pulverized *Zuiho*. Leyte Gulf was a disastrous engagement for the Japanese. In the follow-up actions, which lasted until 27 October, they would lose three more light cruisers to US submarines.

◆ *see* Kamikaze Attacks on Leyte Gulf p. 265

KAMIKAZE ATTACKS ON LEYTE GULF (25–29 OCTOBER 1944)

The Battle of Leyte Gulf and its aftermath were marked by an enormous number of kamikaze attacks on US vessels. The worst occurred on 25 October, when land-based aircraft attacked the USS *Santee*, the USS *Suwannee* and the USS *St Lô*. All were hit by suicide aircraft, the latter sinking at 11:15. Five minutes previously the USS *Kalinin Bay* had also been badly damaged. Wave upon wave of Japanese aircraft appeared over the US fleet, oblivious to the anti-aircraft fire and US fighters. Their sole intention was to immolate themselves on the decks of the enemy vessels. The suicide pilots managed to damage seven escort carriers, one light cruiser, eight destroyers, two landing craft and a tanker during the battle.

BURMA-SIAM RAILWAY OPENS (NOVEMBER 1944)

During November the final sections of the notorious Burma-Thailand railway were completed. The railway stretched some 400 km (249 miles) and it was said that each of the sleepers along its track marked the resting place of one of the Allied prisoners of war, or convicts from Southeast Asia who had died during the construction project. The total body count has been estimated at 150,000.

SINKING OF THE *TIRPITZ* (12 NOVEMBER 1944)

By August 1944 the *Tirpitz* had completed its sea trials. It immediately came to the attention of the Allies, who desperately wanted to sink it. The first operation, codenamed Goodwood, involved attacks by Fleet Air Arm. These failed but Operation Paravane was then planned, using Lancaster bombers to hit the *Tirpitz*, now hiding once again in a Norwegian fjord. There were no hits, but it was not long before Operation Catechism was launched on 12 November, when 32 Lancaster bombers appeared over the *Tirpitz* at approximately 09:35. The first bomb was dropped at 09:41 and the vessel was hit at least twice. It began to list and finally went down with 1,000 of her 1,700 crew; the Lancasters suffered no losses.

see Kriegesmarine p. 22

▲ *ABOVE: The German battleship* Tirpitz *sinks.*

LIBERATION OF ALBANIA (29 NOVEMBER 1944)

On 20 November 1944 the Germans evacuated the Albanian capital of Tirana. On 29 November they evacuated Scutari and moved to link up with Army Group E, which was attempting to hold open the withdrawal route. The evacuation of Albania and Serbia was quickly followed by Bosnia and Herzegovina, with the Germans digging in from Bisegrad, across to the River Drina and to Mostar.

see Soviets Capture Vienna p. 286

HITLER'S LAST GAMBLE (16 DECEMBER 1944)

Originally the last major push by German forces in the west had been fixed to take place on 27 November, but with the latest news, Hitler agreed that it should be postponed until 16 December. With great secrecy and skill the Germans managed to assemble a force of 30 divisions, 2,000 guns, 1,000 tanks and 1,500 aircraft. The divisions alone included 250,000 men. The primary objective was to punch a hole straight through the US lines and effectively cut off the British army advancing in the north. In order to do this, Antwerp would have to be taken and each phase of the operation would be minutely timed. The offensive was also staged at this time of the year to take full advantage of poor weather conditions, eliminating Allied air supremacy. The route the attack would take had in fact been used in 1940 to push the Panzer divisions around the flank of the Maginot Line and it was for this reason that the Ardennes was chosen. The forested area would also provide cover for the German armoured columns. The attack relied on speed, the capture of fuel and no hold ups.

◆ *see* Kampf Gruppe p. 267

KAMPF GRUPPE (16 DECEMBER 1944)

The cream of the carefully husbanded German reserves to be used in the Ardennes offensive was assigned to Kampf Gruppe leader Joachim Peiper. He had 70 tanks at his disposal to reach the River Meuse and open the road into Belgium. His troops moved off at 02:00 on 16 December and almost immediately fell behind schedule after discovering that a vital bridge had been destroyed. He then encountered US opposition – the Americans had been aware of his movements and sought to block him at every point. Peiper's men were caught in a pocket near La Gleize on the afternoon of 18 December and virtually destroyed.

◆ *see* Joachim Peiper p. 268

PEIPER, JOACHIM (1915–76)

Joachim Peiper was born on 30 January 1915, the son of a Prussian officer who had fought in Africa during World War I. He joined the Hitler Youth in 1933, entering the SS the following year. In 1936 he went into officer training and became an officer in the SS. Between 1938 and 1941 he worked as Himmler's adjutant and was probably at least aware of the plans for the Final Solution. He became the commander of the 1st SS Panzer Division and won a Knights Cross at the Battle of Kharkov. At the time of the Ardennes offensive he was a Lieutenant Colonel and spearheaded the offensive. He managed to make the best progress in the entire campaign, covering 100 km (62 miles) in 72 hours, despite the fact that many of his men were untried in battle. He was captured and put on trial at Dachau, where he took full responsibility for what he had done, including the alleged massacre at Malmedy. Nonetheless, he was not sentenced to death and was released from prison in 1956. He died in a house fire on 13 July 1976 – possibly the victim of an arson attack.

see Kampf Gruppe p. 267

LEFT: Joachim Peiper.

OBJECTIVE ANTWERP (DECEMBER 1944)

The primary target of the Ardennes offensive was Antwerp. Once the harbour had been cleared of mines, men and equipment could be brought straight into the city without having to take the tortuous route through France. It was therefore imperative that the Germans denied the Allies the opportunity to take the port. By 20 December German troops had pushed a considerable distance into US-held Belgium and Luxembourg. The high point of the offensive came when the 2nd Panzer Division arrived within range of Dinant on the River Meuse; however, by 20 January the Germans were back at their starting point. The Ardennes offensive cost the Germans 100,000 casualties, 1,000 aircraft and 800 tanks. Allied losses were in excess of 80,000.

◆ *see* Bastogne p. 270

▲ *ABOVE: General Patton's army relieves Bastogne.*

BASTOGNE (DECEMBER 1944)

Bastogne lay at a vital crossroads and in the path of several German Panzer divisions and supporting units. It was effectively surrounded by the night of 24 December, yet despite intense pressure, the hastily scraped together defenders refused to surrender. When requested to surrender by German forces the US commander famously replied 'Nuts'. Bastogne was defended by the 101st Parachute Division and elements of the 9th and 10th divisions under McAuliffe. Patton came to their aid after intense bombardment and attacks on the position.

see Allied Counteroffensive in Ardennes p. 274

MALMEDY MASSACRE (17 DECEMBER 1944)

Elements of the 1st SS Panzer Division approached the Baugnes crossroads near Malmedy, Belgium, encountering a company of the US 7th Armored Division. The US commander, realizing the odds against him, ordered his men to surrender. The troops were searched, marched into a field and shot. Eighty-six were killed, over 40 survived.

see Allies Liberate Buchenwald and Belsen p. 285

SOVIETS REACH BUDAPEST (27 DECEMBER 1944)

By 25 December 1944 Russian troops had reduced the avenue of escape from Budapest to just 16 km (10 miles). By the following day the ring was completed and by 27 December the final stages of the battle for the city had begun. Desperate street fighting continued throughout the city until 13 January 1945 when it was taken by the Russians. The armistice was signed and Hungary declared war on Germany on 21 January.

see Soviets Capture Warsaw p. 275

▶ *RIGHT: Wernher von Braun with a model of his rocket.*

GERMAN ROCKET PROGRAMME (1944–1945)

The Germans had begun experimenting with rocket fuel as early as 1927, and in 1932 the German army had started taking interest, primarily because of its potential for long-range artillery. Werner Von Braun worked on a series of designs which would culminate in the creation of the V2 rocket, which was built by slave labour at a camp called Dora, near Nordhausen in Germany. The first V2 was fired at London on 8 September 1944, the first of some 1,358. Other British targets included Norwich and Ipswich. The Belgian city port of Antwerp received the highest number: 1,610. As it turned out the V2 was militarily ineffective; it was expensive and too primitive to hit specific

targets. The far-more effective machine was the V1, or Buzz Bomb (Doodlebug), of which 30,000 were manufactured, a third of which were fired at Great Britain. They were difficult to shoot down but experienced pilots could tip them off target to land harmlessly in the sea. Ultimately both the V1 and V2 rocket-launching sites were overrun, but not before 3,876 V1s had landed on London alone. One particular pilot, Joseph Berry, accounted for 59 V1 interceptions.

see Werner von Braun p. 203

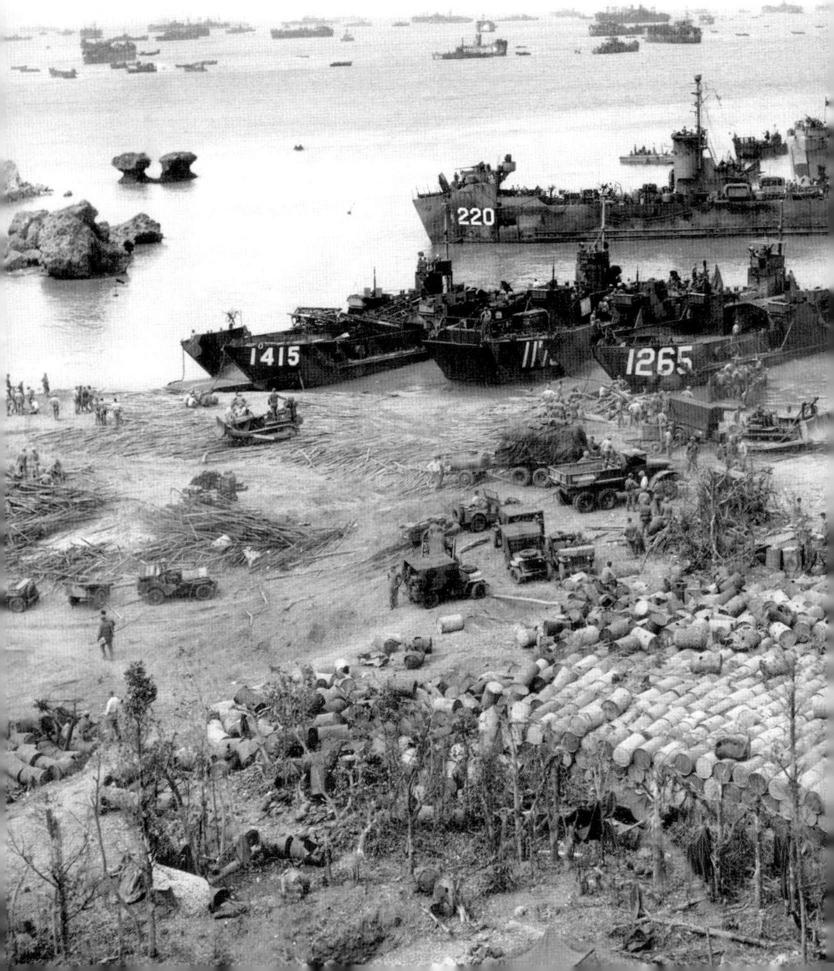
220
1415
1265

1945

OPERATION BODENPLATTE (1 JANUARY 1945)

Operation Bodenplatte was a bold surprise initiative taken by the Luftwaffe on New Years Day 1945. Somehow the Luftwaffe had scraped together 800 aircraft, mainly bombers. The majority were flown by inexperienced pilots, but the targets were Allied airfields in France, Belgium and Holland. The offensive took the Allies completely by surprise, and between 150 and 300 Allied aircraft were lost, mainly on the ground. Irreplaceable Luftwaffe casualties amounted to some 200.

see Dresden p. 277

MARINES LAND ON LUZON (9 JANUARY 1945)

At 09:30 on 9 January, after a vast air and naval bombardment, some 67,000 US troops began landing in the Gulf of Lingayen on the west coast of Luzon. They would face 262,000 Japanese under General Yamashita. The handful of Japanese aircraft made little headway, except for damaging the USS *Mississippi* and the cruiser USS *Columbia*. But the Japanese navy deployed kamikaze boat pilots and managed to sink an American transport ship.

see US Liberates Manila p. 276

ALLIED COUNTEROFFENSIVE IN ARDENNES (9–16 JANUARY 1945)

The US 1st and 3rd Armies were charged with the task of dealing with the salient created by the German Ardennes counteroffensive. All units made good progress and by 16 January the Ardennes salient had been reduced to half its former size. Continued pressure continued until 20 January, when the Germans found themselves where they had started over a month previously. Meanwhile, Patton's 3rd Army was advancing on every front and reached the junction of the Rivers Sauer and Our. On 21 January a new Allied offensive in the St Vith area was planned; this time the weather had improved and there would be good air cover.

CHAFEE (1943–45)

The M24 Chafee was built as a successor to the M5 Stuart light tank in April 1943. Development was led by Cadillac in the US and two .30 calibre machine guns were fitted, one on the right front of the hull, the other alongside the main armament in the mantlet. A third machine gun was also fitted on the cupola. It had the same engine as the M5 Stuart light tank, with over 3,000 being produced before the end of hostilities. The M24 saw service with the US army's reconnaissance and light-tank battalions throughout Europe and in the Pacific. The tank was also supplied to the British army, who nicknamed it the Chafee, a name which the Americans themselves adopted for the tank after the war had ended. The M24 was considered to be a reliable, manoeuvrable and fast vehicle. The standard M24 would not only be one of the first western Allied tanks to cross the Rhine, and would still be in use during the Korean War, but also remained in many armies throughout the world for a number of years after the war, still regarded as an extremely versatile and reliable vehicle.

◀ see Bridge at Remagen p. 279

SOVIETS CAPTURE WARSAW (17 JANUARY 1945)

The Russians allowed the Polish 1st Army to launch the final offensive against Warsaw. Very few people had managed to live among the ruins

▲ *ABOVE: The capture of Warsaw.*

and after the Warsaw uprising the Germans had deported 600,000 people to concentration camps. By 18 January the last Germans had been driven from Warsaw and the Russians began their advance out of Poland and towards the German border.

US LIBERATES MANILA (3 FEBRUARY 1945)
Elements of the 1st Cavalry Division managed to reach the outskirts of Manila, supported by the 37th Division on 3 February 1945. The following day they began patrols in the area. On 5 February the last of the Japanese began to withdraw from the northern outskirts of the capital and MacArthur ordered his men forward to seize the city. Cleaning-up exercises continued for a number of days and Japanese counterattacks were repulsed.

◘ *see* Iwo Jima p. 278

YALTA CONFERENCE (4–11 FEBRUARY 1945)
At the Yalta Conference, which opened on 4 February 1945, Churchill, Roosevelt and Stalin reached agreement on the remaining war strategy and the post-war world. Russia agreed to turn against Japan as soon as Germany had been conquered. Although the two western Allies were concerned about the power Stalin might wield in the post-war years, they had little choice but to concede further allowances in the Far East to him in order to ensure his support. In effect Russia and the US carved up the world between them and Churchill was powerless to block their intentions. Amongst the many contentious issues were Russian or Eastern European citizens who had been captured in German uniform by the western Allies. Stalin demanded that they be returned.

◘ *see* Unconditional German Surrender p. 294

DRESDEN (13–14 FEBRUARY 1945)

At 22:15 on 13 February a formation of 244 Lancaster bombers began dropping incendiaries on the major German city of Dresden. Three hours later, a larger force hit Dresden again. The city was aflame, but at 12:00 on 14 February a vast armada of US B-17 bombers dropped tons of high explosives on the shattered city. The Germans claimed 70,000 had perished in the bombings (later reappraised at 250,000). Allied estimates, based on Russian figures, placed around 320,000 dead, although more contemporary evidence puts the figure at no more than 35,000.

◆ see Raid on Bershtesgaden p. 286

▲ *ABOVE: Churchill, Roosevelt and Stalin at the Yalta Conference.*

IWO JIMA (19 FEBRUARY–26 MARCH 1945)

Iwo Jima was a tiny island, but an important asset for whoever could control it – from here bombers could rain terror on the Japanese mainland. The Japanese had mustered 22,000 men for its defence and they had spent months building strong points and bomb-proof positions. Landings commenced on 19 February and from the outset met heavy opposition from the Japanese. By the end of the first day the marines had taken over 2,000 casualties, but they had cut the island in two. Although the US flag was raised on Mount Suribachi on 23 February, the battle was by no means over. Fresh American reserves had landed and by 11 March the last Japanese survivors were holding Kitano Point at the island's northernmost tip. Of the 22,000 Japanese only 212 were captured; the rest had been killed. US dead and wounded had topped 26,000.

see Okinawa p. 283

▲ *ABOVE: Troops heading for Iwo Jima.*

TOKYO FIREBOMB RAID (25 FEBRUARY 1945)

The US Air Force XXI Bomber Group, flying B-29 Super Fortresses, carried out a devastating firebomb raid on Tokyo on 25 February. Around 170 aircraft dropped incendiary bombs on the largely wooden capital of Japan. A square mile of the city was devastated. On the same day carrier-born aircraft precision bombed Japanese airfields and aircraft factories. The procedure was repeated the following day, again over Tokyo.

◈ *see* Tokyo Air Raid p. 280

BRIDGE AT REMAGEN (7 MARCH 1945)

On the same day that the US 3rd Armoured Division captured Cologne, elements of the 9th Armoured succeeded in establishing bridgeheads across the Rhine and the Ahr. The most stunning coup of the day was the capture of the Remagen Bridge. It had been the American intention to destroy the bridge and cut off German troops trapped west of the Rhine. However, seeing it intact made them change their operational plans and they immediately threw troops across the bridge, switching their whole axis of attack. News of the disaster reached a furious Hitler, who immediately

▶ RIGHT: *Collapse of the Remagen bridge.*

sacked von Rundstedt (Commander-in-Chief of German forces in the west). Hitler said of von Rundstedt 'He is finished. I don't want to hear any more about him.' Kesselring was recalled to take up the position. Over the next two days some 300 Luftwaffe bombers attempted to destroy the bridge, but they failed. By now thousands of Allied troops had crossed the Rhine and were taking up strong positions in the newly gained bridgehead. By 11 March cleaning-up exercises to the west of the river were all but over.

see The Pershing p. 280

THE PERSHING (1945)

The Pershing tank received its baptism of fire at Remagen on 7 March 1945. The tank would see limited service during the war but it was well matched against the best of the German tanks. The Pershing had a 90-mm gun and a 500 hp engine, meaning that it could achieve speeds of 48 km (30 mph). It had arrived in the European Theatre rather too late to have any significant impact; however, in the summer of 1945 it was deployed against the Japanese on Okinawa. The Pershing remained in US military service and saw considerable action during the Korean War. At last the US had created a tank which was the equal of any other vehicle in either the Axis or Allied armouries. Had it been available earlier, it would have made a significant impact on the progress of the war.

see Operation Varsity p. 282

TOKYO AIR RAID (9 MARCH 1945)

In a combined operation, 334 B-29 bombers, flying out of Guam, Saipan and Tinian, launched a three-hour incendiary bomb raid on Tokyo on

▶ *RIGHT: Extensive bomb damage in Tokyo after the B-29 raids.*

9 March. Ten square miles, a full fifth of the total area of the city, was razed to the ground. Japanese sources admitted to 130,000 dead, although other figures suggest it could have been as high as 200,000. If the Japanese had thought conventional weapons were devastating, the worse was yet to come.

◆ *see* Japanese Government Collapses p. 284

OPERATION VARSITY (24–25 MARCH 1945)

On the morning of 24 March 1945, an enormous air armada of 3,000 aircraft and gliders passed over the River Rhine and began dropping 14,000 paratroopers of the British 6th Airborne and the US 17th Airborne Division. The armada took 2.5 hours to pass over the Rhine; it was supported by nearly 900 US and RAF fighter aircraft. The paratroopers were dropped around Wesel, with instruction to link up with the British 2nd Army forces. By the evening they had captured all their key objectives and had penetrated 10 km (6 miles) into German territory. The operation had been meticulously planned and was, in many respects, exactly what Arnhem should have been. By this stage German troops were increasingly unable to respond rapidly to any growing danger, due to the immediate interdiction from Allied air superiority.

By 26 March the airborne units had extended their area of occupation and were advancing rapidly. By 29 March elements of the 2nd British Army had reached Osnabruck. By early April XXX Corps had managed to reach the Dortmund-Ems Canal. British forces were closing their side of a vast salient that had developed in the Ruhr, which was being exploited by the US 1st Army.

■ see The Ruhr Pocket p. 282

THE RUHR POCKET (1 APRIL 1945)

By 1 April 1945, with Canadian troops having advanced beyond Osnabruck, elements of the British army linked up with the US 9th and 1st Armies at Lippstadt, effectively closing off the Ruhr region. The whole of Army Group B and two corps of the 1st Parachute Army were trapped in a 113-km (70-mile) pocket located

between the Rivers Rhine and Ruhr. The pocket stretched 80 km (50 miles) from the River Sieg to the River Lippe. Over the next couple of days the British added their weight to the offensive and the Americans consolidated their position. On 4 April pressure was applied from both the north and the south and a new offensive was opened two days later. By 14 April the bulk of the pocket had been pierced and the Germans were on the verge of losing another 300,000 men. By now events were overtaking issues on the Ruhr; western Allied thrusts had passed Hanover and Leipzig and the German front in Italy had collapsed. In the east the situation was worse and within days both Vienna and Berlin would fall and Hitler would be dead.

see Allies Meet on the Elbe p. 287

OKINAWA (1 APRIL–22 JUNE 1945)

US intelligence believed that the garrison on Okinawa was 65,000-strong but it was in fact double this figure. The job of taking the island fell to the 10th Army and its 180,000 men. The main landing on 1 April was preceded by a huge bombardment and during this time the Japanese launched 193 kamikaze missions against the fleet.

LEFT: The beachhead at Okinawa.

Regardless, the US was able to land 60,000 men on the first day. The island was fanatically defended and as the Americans advanced, the Japanese launched a series of costly counterattacks. The main Japanese defence lines were pierced on 24 April but they ran into a second line of defence four days later. Throughout April more kamikaze missions were launched and by the end of the month over 3,000 of these attacks had been made; the US had lost 21 ships as a result. On 21 May the Japanese began to fall back from their last defence line, but it was not until 22 June that the last resistance was crushed. Indeed Okinawa was not secure until 2 July. The Japanese had lost 107,500 killed and significantly, 7,400 taken prisoner.

see Allies Deliver an Ultimatum to Japan p. 300

SOVIETS DENOUNCE THE PACT WITH JAPAN (5 APRIL 1945)

With the war in Europe rapidly spinning out of German control, the Russian government informed the Japanese Ambassador in Moscow that they intended to denounce their five-year non-aggression pact, which had been signed in 1941. Stalin had already moved considerable military assets east in order to exploit Japan's worsening position in the Pacific and the imminent US attacks on their mainland.

see Soviet Union Declares War on Japan p. 302

JAPANESE GOVERNMENT COLLAPSES (5 APRIL 1945)

Facing the threat of Russia as well as Britain and the US, the government of General Kuniaki Koiso realized it was finished. Koiso resigned and a new government was formed under Admiral Kantaro Suzuki. On 7 April, the Japanese attacked the US in the battle of the East China Sea. The Japanese ships were overwhelmed and the *Yamato* was sunk.

see US Plans to Invade the Japanese Mainland p. 296

▲ ABOVE: The Japanese battleship Yamato, sunk in the East China Sea.

ALLIES LIBERATE BUCHENWALD AND BELSEN (11–13 APRIL 1945)

In their offensive into the Weimar sector the US 3rd Army stumbled on Buchenwald and Bad Sulza, two extensive German concentration camps. On 13 April, as British troops drove towards Bremen and sought to cross the River Leine, they crossed the Luneberg Heath and discovered the Nazi concentration camp at Belsen. At Belsen the British found 40,000 prisoners on the verge of death and thousands of rotting corpses. Even after the liberation, around 600 died every day. At Buchenwald the US troops rushed food and medical supplies to the 20,000 survivors. Thousands more of them would die within days of liberation.

◆ see Dachau is Liberated p. 289

SOVIETS CAPTURE VIENNA (13 APRIL 1945)

After seven years of German occupation, Vienna fell to Russian troops at around 14:00 on 13 April after several days savage fighting. Ironically, the last German stand in Vienna was in the old Jewish quarter. Their choice of this location saved many of Vienna's most important historic buildings. At the end of the fighting the Russians had netted 130,000 prisoners. On 15 April, Hitler uselessly bragged 'Berlin is still German, Vienna will return to Germany'. Already the Russians were preparing for the final push on Berlin and had amassed 1.6 million men, 3,827 tanks, over 2,000 self-propelled guns, 4,500 anti-tank guns, 15,500 field guns, 6,700 aircraft and 96,000 other vehicles. To oppose these the Germans had just 47 divisions.

◗ *see* Allies Meet on the Elbe p. 287

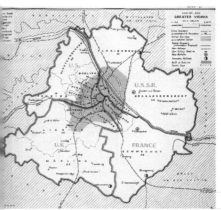

◀ *LEFT: Map showing Allied occupied zones.*

RAID ON BERSHTESGADEN (24 APRIL 1945)

The RAF Bomber Command launched their last major operation against Hitler's mountain residence of Bershtesgaden on 24 April 1945. They failed to catch Hitler there, but ironically only one day before, after six years, the blackout in London was lifted. Hitler had officially taken over the defence of Berlin. He was in charge of 300,000 men and women whom he exhorted to defend the capital to the very last.

◗ *see* Food not Bombs p. 288

ALLIES MEET ON THE ELBE (25 APRIL 1945)

As Anglo-American and Russian troops cut through Germany, they first met at Torgau on the River Elbe. To the north US troops were reaching Russian lines on the Baltic coast. Across Germany white flags hung from windows and the Allies were having difficulty dealing with the number of refugees, not to mention the one million German prisoners captured by the western Allies alone in the last three weeks.

◆ *see* Doenitz Takes Control p. 291

PÉTAIN FAILS TO ESCAPE TO SWITZERLAND (26 APRIL 1945)

Pétain had been arrested by the Germans on 20 August 1944 after refusing to stand down. He had been taken to Belfort, but on 1 October he was removed from there and taken to Sigmaringen in Germany. On 26 April Pétain was arrested attempting to cross the Swiss border from France. Subsequently he was tried for treason and sentenced to death – later commuted to life imprisonment.

◆ *see* Mussolini and his Mistress are Assassinated p. 288

▶ *RIGHT: Marshal Pétain.*

FOOD NOT BOMBS (28 APRIL 1944)

In response to the privations being suffered in Holland, notably a grave shortage in food, US B-17 Flying Fortresses and RAF Bomber Command Lancasters appeared over the cities of The Hague, Rotterdam and other major centres. On this occasion their cargoes did not rain death, but instead contained vital food parcels and medical supplies for the starving Dutch. By May food was routinely being brought into Holland by truck.

see Unconditional German Surrender p. 294

MUSSOLINI AND HIS MISTRESS ARE ASSASSINATED (28 APRIL 1945)

Mussolini and his mistress, Clara Petacci, were arrested and tried by the partisans on 28 April. Mussolini was found hiding under a pile of coats in a convoy of cars. He immediately surrendered and after a brief trial was condemned to death. The sentence was immediately carried out along with his mistress and 12 other fascist leaders. Their bodies were taken to Milan where they were hung up on display.

see Hitler and his Inner Circle Commit Suicide p. 290

HITLER AND EVA BRAUN MARRY (29 APRIL 1945)

Determined to remain in Berlin until the bitter end, Hitler gave orders that the struggle should continue in southern Germany in what he believed to be an alpine fortress. His major act of the day, however, was to marry his long-term mistress, Eva Braun. They wed in a bunker beneath the shattered streets of Berlin.

see Hitler and his Inner Circle Commit Suicide p. 290

▶ RIGHT: Hitler and his mistress Eva Braun at their Bavarian retreat.

DACHAU IS LIBERATED (29 APRIL 1945)

Several different US army units claim to have liberated the Dachau concentration camp. What is certain was the impact of seeing thousands of starving prisoners and thousands more dead; a line of cattle trucks alone contained the bodies of over 2,300 Hungarian and Polish Jews. SS Guards were treated roughly and it has been suggested that up to 500 of them were executed on the spot by vengeful US troops.

◆ *see* Post-War Legacy p. 306

HITLER AND HIS INNER CIRCLE COMMIT SUICIDE (30 APRIL 1945)

At approximately 15:30 on 30 April 1945, Adolf Hitler committed suicide, having taken the life of Eva Braun, whom he had married just the previous day, prior to turning the gun on himself. He had given up hope that any German troops would be able to save Berlin. Indeed, at 22:50 that night advanced units of the Russian 150th Infantry Division stormed the Reichstag and planted the hammer and sickle on its roof.

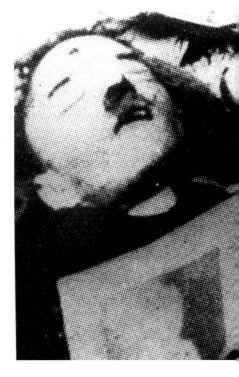

There was mass panic in the Führer bunker and Goebbels had his whole family killed before taking his own life. Many of the inner circle either jockeyed for position in the dying embers of the German empire or simply disappeared. Key figures such as Himmler and Goering would later be picked up, but others, including Bormann were never positively identified.

◨ *see* Doenitz Takes Control p. 291

DOENITZ TAKES CONTROL (1 MAY 1945)

On 1 May 1945, the official announcement of Hitler's death reached the German public. He had appointed Doenitz as his legal successor. Grand Admiral Karl Doenitz, speaking on Hamburg radio, assured the German people that the struggle would go on. In truth few Germans believed him as the situation was worse than critical. In effect there was no longer an Eastern and Western Front; they had merged into one and small groups of German units now concentrated on trying to struggle westward in order to avoid falling into the hands of the Russians. There was no more chance of defending the soil of Germany when the prospect of a Siberian labour camp beckoned. Doenitz had his own plans for Germany.

see Karl Doenitz p. 292

▲ ABOVE: Hitler shot his wife of one day, Eva Braun, before committing suicide.

DOENITZ, KARL (1891–1980)

Doenitz was commissioned a naval officer in 1913, serving in submarines and surface vessels during World War I. In 1935 he took control of the German U-boat fleets. Lacking sufficient submarines, Doenitz carried out widespread attacks on Allied shipping between 1940 and 1943. Doenitz became head of the German navy (1943), replacing Erich Raeder, but the naval war had turned against Germany and by mid-1943, the battle for the Atlantic was lost.

Despite increasing submarine production from 1943, German naval forces' resistance had collapsed by 1945. Hitler appointed Doenitz his successor just before committing suicide. Doenitz negotiated Germany's surrender on 8 May, was tried at Nuremberg, and received 10 years imprisonment. He was released in October 1956 and wrote his autobiography, published in 1959. Doenitz died on 24 December 1980.

◆ *see* Unconditional German Surrender p. 294

◀ LEFT: *Grand Admiral Doenitz.*

FALL OF BERLIN (1 MAY 1945)

As over a million German troops began surrendering in Italy and Austria, General Krebs, the senior German officer in Berlin, was told by the Russians to accept unconditional surrender. At this stage both Bormann and Goebbels were alive and determined to continue the struggle, but General Weidling, the garrison commander, decided on a surrender. Bormann disappeared, whilst Goebbels and his family and Krebs committed suicide. The order to surrender went out to Berlin but still-fanatical Nazis continued to resist within the city. There was no thought or concern for the 150,000 German troops that surrounded them in Yugoslavia. The following day Russian troops concentrated on clearing opposition in the capital and isolated pockets of resistance still remained.

GERMANS SURRENDER IN ITALY (2 MAY 1945)

The German situation in Italy had become untenable and Colonel Schweinitz, representative of General Vietinghoff signed an unconditional surrender, effective from 13:00 hours on 2 May 1945. The surrender document encompassed all German troops under his command in Italy. On the same day, however, US troops reached Milan, which had already been liberated by anti-Fascist Partisans. The following day Turin fell.

RANGOON IS LIBERATED (3 MAY 1945)

On 1 May the British launched Operation Dracula and two Ghurka parachute battalions were dropped on the mouth of the Irrawaddy River to the south of Rangoon. On 3 May they linked up with the 20th Indian Division advancing down the Irrawaddy Valley. The Japanese evacuated Rangoon just as the 26th Indian Division liberated the city. There were, however, still some isolated Japanese troops to be dealt with in Burma.

◆ see US Plans to Invade the Japanese Mainland p. 296

UNCONDITIONAL GERMAN SURRENDER (4 MAY 1945)

On Doenitz's instructions, General Von Friedberg signed the unconditional surrender document at 18:20, authorizing the capitulation of all armed forces in Holland, north-west Germany and Denmark. The document was signed at General Montgomery's headquarters at Luneberg Heath. The full surrender took place at 02:41 in a schoolhouse in Rheims, when Jodl, the German army Chief of Staff, signed the full unconditional surrender document before General Eisenhower. Jodl commented 'With this signature, the German people and the German armed forces are, for better or for worse, delivered into the victor's hands.' The Germans had delayed the full surrender to allow as many of their troops to struggle westward as possible. The real surrender had occurred with the signature at Montgomery's

▲ *ABOVE: Field Marshall Wilhelm Keitel signs the surrender to the Red Army on 9 May 1945.*

headquarters, but now this unconditional surrender had been made in the presence of the representatives of Britain, Russia and the US. Across Europe the relief was almost tangible. After six years of war, the privations were temporarily forgotten in a blaze of fireworks and flags.

◀ *see* Goergy Zhukov p. 295

ZHUKOV, GEORGY (1896–1974)

Zhukov served in the Imperial Russian Army during World War I and joined the Communists in 1917, serving as a cavalry commander. Interested in armoured warfare, his knowledge convinced Stalin to appoint him Chief of Staff in 1940. Zhukov, unable to prevent the slaughter and surrender of Russian troops in the early years, saved Moscow. He rebuilt the Russian army and after Stalingrad transformed the machines that fought to Hitler's door. He was accorded the title, the 'man who never lost a battle'.

Stalin sidelined Zhukov after 1945, but he returned on the leader's death in 1953, becoming First Deputy Minister for Defence (1955) then a member of the Executive Committee of the Communist Party (1957). Sacked in 1957 for placing the military above the party, he spent the 1960s writing and died in 1974.

◄► see Potsdam Conference p. 300

▶ RIGHT: Georgy Zhukov.

CHINESE TAKE FOOCHOW AND NANNING (18–26 MAY 1945)

In the Fukien Province, Chinese forces reoccupied Foochow and additional Chinese divisions, engaged and fighting in Burma, began moving back towards China on 18 May 1945. On 26 May the Japanese evacuated Nanning, the capital of Kwangsi Province. This meant that the Japanese no longer had an overland communication route with Indo-China. On 7 June the Chinese launched a major operation to assist in liberating Hong Kong and Canton.

BRITISH CAPTURE HIMMLER (22 MAY 1945)

Himmler was arrested in Bremen on 22 May, disguised as a German military policeman. He was taken into immediate custody and was due to stand trial with other prominent Nazi leaders as a war criminal at Nuremberg, but he had secreted a cyanide capsule which he took before his British captors could interrogate him. Even to his death Himmler remained an unrepentant Nazi.

◆ *see* British Capture Von Ribbentrop p. 296

US PLANS TO INVADE THE JAPANESE MAINLAND (25 MAY 1945)

On 25 May the US military began consideration of the proposed invasion of the Japanese mainland. A series of documents were produced between May and June 1945. Over the previous six months 300,000 Japanese had been killed during bombings. The Joint Chiefs of Staff set the invasion of Kyushu (Operation Olympic) for 1 December 1945 and the island of Honshu (Operation Coronet) for 1 March 1946.

TOKYO IS FIREBOMBED (24–26 MAY 1945)

On 24 May 520 American bombers dropped 3,500 tons of bombs on the centre of Tokyo and industrial areas to the south. The bombers were back on 26 May; this time they dropped 3,252 tons of bombs on the Ginza district and areas adjacent to the Imperial Palace. By this stage Japanese war production was down to 20 per cent.

◆ *see* Allies Deliver an Ultimatum to the Japanese p. 300

BRITISH CAPTURE VON RIBBENTROP (10 JUNE 1945)

Von Ribbentrop was captured by British troops on 10 June 1945. He was one of the key figures being sought by the Allies. As it transpired at Nuremberg, he was active in the planning of the attack on Poland, the framing of the Final Solution and conspiracies ending in the murder of Allied prisoners of war. Von Ribbentrop claimed that he was carrying out Hitler's orders.

➤ *see* Joachim von Rippentrop p. 297

RIBBENTROP, JOACHIM VON (1893–1946)

Ribbentrop was awarded the Iron Cross during World War I, but after hostilities ended he returned to civilian life. Joining the Nazi Party in May 1932 and becoming Hitler's foreign affairs advisor, Ribbentrop was appointed Ambassador to London in 1936 and Foreign Minister in 1938. He was involved in negotiations with the British and French during the late 1930s and the German-Soviet Pact of 1939. Trying to placate the Russians, Ribbentrop telegrammed Molotov saying the German-Japanese pact was aimed at the US, not Russia. Ribbentrop faded into the background during the remainder of the war, yet the Allies were convinced he was implicated in

▲ *ABOVE: Joachim von Ribbentrop.*

German racial policies and war crimes. He was tried and convicted at Nuremberg, and sentenced to death; his execution was carried out on 16 October 1946.

➤ *see* Nuremberg Trials p. 304

CHINESE KEEP UP THE PRESSURE (1 JULY 1945)

On 1 July the Chinese liberated Liuchow and on 27 July they began a month-long battle for the possession of Kweilin. Meanwhile, on 5 August the Chinese 13th Army captured Tanchuk and the 58th Division Hsinning. By 12 August it was clear that the Japanese were on the verge of surrender and consequently the Chinese decided to cancel their intended invasion of Hong Kong and Canton.

◆ see Soviet Union Declares War on Japan p. 302

CHURCHILL LOSES THE ELECTION (5 JULY 1945)

The results of the 5 July General Election in Britain were declared on 26 July. It was a landslide victory for the Labour Party with 393 seats against the Conservative's 213. Churchill was shaken by the result. He was quoted as saying 'The decision has been recorded. I have therefore laid down the charge which was placed upon me in darker times. It only remains for me to express my profound gratitude for the unflinching support they have given their servant through these perilous years.' The new Prime Minister, Clement Attlee, said of the victory 'We are facing a new era. Labour can deliver the goods.' By 27 July Attlee was in the thick of it at the Potsdam Conference.

◆ see Potsdam Conference p. 300

FIRST ATOMIC BOMB IS DETONATED AT LOS ALAMOS (16 JULY 1941)

On 16 July, at 17:30 at Los Alamos in New Mexico, the first atomic bomb was successfully detonated. The project to develop the weapon had been completed by an international team of scientists. Within a matter of days an additional weapon would be created that would hasten the end of Japan's resistance. Scientists worked around the clock to ensure completion.

�« see Manhattan Project p. 299

MANHATTAN PROJECT (1942–45)

In the 1930s it became clear that the Germans were working on an atomic bomb. They had developed a heavy water plant and high-grade uranium and were already working on associated issues. In the US the major effort to create an atomic bomb got underway in 1942. The primary laboratory was in Los Alamos under the direction of Robert Oppenheimer. There was a great need for secrecy, yet speed was also of the essence. Whilst the Manhattan Project continued apace, British special-operations executive agents managed to destroy a vital factory in Norway that the Germans needed to build their atomic bomb. The Germans quickly rebuilt it and in November 1943 it was destroyed once again, this time by American bombers. Scientists working on the Manhattan Project managed to complete three bombs, the first of which was tested at Los Alamos, New Mexico on 16 July 1945. They had intended to use it on Germany but Truman changed the target to Japan. Certainly the use of the bombs at Hiroshima and Nagasaki hastened the end of the war by at least six months.

�« see Hiroshima p. 301

◀ *LEFT: The new British Prime Minister Clement Attlee, who defeated Churchill.*

POTSDAM CONFERENCE (17 JULY–2 AUGUST 1945)

The Potsdam Conference opened on 17 July 1945. Central to the discussions there was the situation in Europe and possible solutions to bring a swift end to the war against Japan. There was severe disagreement about the territorial boundaries of Germany. Stalin refused to allow free elections in Eastern Europe and brushed aside criticisms of the situation in many of these countries. It was Churchill who coined the

▲ *ABOVE: Churchill, Truman and Stalin at the Potsdam Conference.*

term 'Iron Curtain', as he felt that Stalin was excluding the West from all decisions related to Eastern Europe. Significantly Roosevelt, who had died in April, had been replaced by President Truman and Churchill was replaced by Attlee during the conference; only Stalin remained of the original three.

◆ *see* Japanese Surrender p. 304

ALLIES DELIVER AN ULTIMATUM TO THE JAPANESE (26 JULY 1945)

During the Potsdam Conference the Allies issued a proclamation demanding Japan's unconditional surrender. Although officially Stalin was unaware of the atomic bomb, his intelligence services had warned him of the development and he was aware of the implications of the surrender demand.

JAPAN REJECTS THE ULTIMATUM (30 JULY 1945)

Japan formally rejected the Potsdam ultimatum. Nonetheless, in anticipation of what would soon befall Japan, General MacArthur and Admiral Nimitz began to prepare their plans for the immediate surrender of the Japanese. Meanwhile conventional warfare continued with increasingly desperate kamikaze attacks on US shipping near Okinawa. The US responded by bombarding airfields and industrial targets across Japan. The US attacks continued until 1 August then ceased.

◆ *see* Hiroshima p. 301

HIROSHIMA (6 AUGUST 1941)

At 09:30 on 6 August 1945 a B-29 bomber, the Enola Gay, dropped the first atomic bomb on a live target. The bomb, which was the equivalent of 20,000 tons of high explosive, flattened the city of Hiroshima in Japan. More than 92,000 people were killed instantly, 37,425 more injured, many of whom would die agonizing deaths over the next decade and more. The decision to

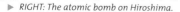

▶ RIGHT: *The atomic bomb on Hiroshima.*

drop the bomb had not been an easy one, but Truman saw this as a means to avoid a potentially ruinous invasion of Japan. Japan had been trying to seek a negotiated peace, but it could not accept unconditional surrender as this would impact upon Emperor Hirohito. The choice of target had also been difficult to make. Originally the favoured target was Kyoto but due to its historical importance Hiroshima had moved to the top of the list. Truman issued the order to drop the bomb on 25 July after the US army's strategic airforces in the Pacific requested a written authorization.

B-29 (1945)

The B-29 was the most expensive weapon created by the US during the war. Some 4,000 were used in the Pacific alone. They were mass-assembled in various US cities including Seattle, Washington and New Jersey. The aircraft had a maximum speed of 576 kph (360 mph) and a range of 5230 km (3,250 miles). They were capable of carrying a vast payload. Today only one airworthy B-29 Super Fortress remains in existence, although several are being restored.

◆ *see* Hiroshima p. 301

SOVIET UNION DECLARES WAR ON JAPAN (8 AUGUST 1945)

The successful dropping of the first atomic bomb on Hiroshima made the future seem bleak for the Japanese – they had no weapon that could match the destructive power of that now wielded by the Allies. But there was worse to come. The Russians, having repudiated their non-aggression pact with Japan on 5 April 1945, stepped up the pressure by declaring war. The implications were far-reaching and Japan knew that Russia would soon mobilize against them.

◆ *see* Japanese Surrender p. 304

NAGASAKI (9 AUGUST 1945)

On 9 August the US B-29 Great Artist dropped a second atomic bomb – Fat Man – on Nagasaki, a major ship-building centre. In seconds, between 25,000 and 70,000 people were killed and a further 43,000 injured. Truman gave the sternest warning 'If Japan does not surrender, atomic bombs will be dropped on her war industries – a rain or ruin from the air, the like of which has never been seen on this earth'. Churchill was more philosophical and said 'By God's mercy, British and American science outpaced all German efforts. The possession of these powers by the Germans at any time might have altered the result of the war and profound anxiety was felt by those who were informed.'

▲ ABOVE: The result of the bomb on Nagasaki.

JAPAN ACCEPTS AN UNCONDITIONAL SURRENDER (14 AUGUST 1945)

With great reluctance, Emperor Hirohito accepted an unconditional surrender on 14 August 1945, but 11:00 1,000 troops attacked the Imperial Palace to prevent him from transmitting the message; they were driven off. The US received the news and prepared to begin the occupation of Japan. The news took some time to filter through to Japanese combat units and it was several days before mass surrenders begin to take place.

JAPANESE SURRENDER (2 SEPTEMBER 1945)

Aboard the USS *Missouri* anchored in Tokyo Bay, the Japanese Foreign Minister and Chief of Staff, Woshijiro Umezo, signed the unconditional surrender document at 08:00 in the presence of General MacArthur. MacArthur was there to represent the Allies, but he had ensured that the US General Wainwright, from Bataan and the British General Percival, captured at Singapore, were both on hand to witness the historic signing. The document was ratified on behalf of the US by Admiral Nimitz, Admiral Bruce Fraser for Great Britain, General Blamey for Australia, General Hsu Yung-chang for China, General Kuzma Derebianko for Russia, Admiral Helfrich for Holland, General Leclerc for France, Colonel Moore-Cosgrave for Canada and Air Marshall Leonard Isitt for New Zealand. MacArthur stated after the signing ceremony 'It is my earnest hope, and indeed the hope of all mankind that from this solemn occasion a better world shall emerge out of the blood and carnage of the past'. Clement Attlee spoke at midnight in Britain saying 'Japan has today surrendered. The last of our enemies is laid low.' Truman addressed the crowds from the White House and said 'This is the day we have been waiting for since Pearl Harbor'.

◆ *see* The Post-War Legacy p. 306

NUREMBERG TRIALS (20 NOVEMBER 1945–OCTOBER 1946)

Twenty-two of the key Nazi figures were tried by an international military tribunal at Nuremberg from 20 November 1945. The tribunal had representatives of the British, Russian, American and French governments. The Nazis were all charged on four counts: conspiracy to wage war; crimes against peace; war crimes; and crimes against humanity. The sentences were as follows: Martin Bormann death by hanging; Karl Doenitz 10 years imprisonment; Hans Frank death by

▲ ABOVE: Japan signs an unconditional surrender to to the Allies.

hanging; Wilhelm Frick death by hanging; Hans Fritzsche was acquitted; Walther Funk life imprisonment; Hermann Goering death by hanging; Rudolf Hess life imprisonment; Alfred Jodl death by hanging; Ernst Kaltenbrunner death by hanging; Wilhelm Keitel death by hanging; Erich Raeder life imprisonment; Alfred Rosenberg death by hanging; Fritz Sauckel death by hanging; Hjalmar Schacht acquitted; Arthur Seyss-Inquart death by hanging; Alfred Speer 20 years; Julius Streicher death by hanging; Konstantine von Neurath 15 years; Franz von Papen acquitted; Joachim von Ribbentrop death by hanging; and Baldur von Schirach 20 years. Some, however, did not have their sentence carried out. Goering would cheat the hangman by swallowing poison. Rudolf Hess would commit suicide in prison in 1987 and von Neurath served just eight years of his sentence.

◆ see The Post-War Legacy p. 306

THE POST-WAR LEGACY

The peace of 1945 had sought to settle many of the issues that had been the root cause of war in 1939. In reality, however, the end of World War II posed more questions and potential problems than it had resolved. One of the first major problems was the loss of power and prestige for the French. They had for a period of time lost the ability to control their empire and what was more, their empire in the Far East had suffered enormously during Japanese occupation. This would leave a smouldering ember that would eventually spark the Vietnam War.

In Europe, no sooner had the Potsdam Conference broken up than the shutters came down, pitting East against West for 40 years. It was only after the economic collapse of the Soviet Union, long after the death of Stalin, that many countries in Eastern Europe could once again move towards democracy.

The impact on Britain was perhaps the most severe. Although it had not been occupied by Germany, its far-flung possessions had either been menaced or taken during the six years of the war. Economically the country was ruined, owing billions to its banker, the United States. Whilst many European countries enjoyed the benefits of post-war programmes to rebuild what had been destroyed during the war, it was notable that Britain, as a victor, received little or none of this assistance.

At least two more legacies remained to haunt the world. The state of Yugoslavia, which had fought amongst itself as much as against its occupiers during the war, did not last much beyond the death of Tito. Each formerly independent state splintered down ethnic lines, causing death and destruction on a scale not seen in Europe since the war itself. Most recently the post-war legacy has brought two separate conflicts to the Middle East. In reparation for the suffering of Jews in Europe, many nations supported the creation of the state of Israel, which has been at loggerheads with its neighbours since the 1940s. Equally, in Iraq – a country whose borders were determined primarily by the British – ethnic differences led to the domination of one group over another for several decades before finally, in 2003, two long-term allies, Britain and the US had to step in and deal with the issue.

There have been various estimates of the number of deaths directly attributed to World War II. Conservatively, the total can be put at just over 56 million worldwide. Russia and China suffered worst, with 21.3 million and 11.3 million respectively. Germany had lost just over seven million, a similar number to Poland. Even countries whose territory was never threatened to any great degree, such as Australia, New Zealand, South Africa and Canada, all lost tens of thousands.

◀ *LEFT: The D-Day landings in June 1944.*

As 1939 creeps to within 70 years of present day, there are precious few World War II veterans left alive. Only the youngest, or those who experienced the final few years of the war now remain. Their dwindling numbers have not diminished the pride and the sorrow of remembrance. True history, it has been said, applies only to times that are sufficiently distant in the memory, and where none remain who personally experienced that age. All too soon the veterans who personally experienced World War II will also be gone.

Without doubt World War II represented a truly global conflict in a far more significant and all-encompassing manner than any other conflict before it. Although World War I had seen horrendous carnage on the Western Front and in the East, elsewhere in the world the conflict had been restricted to a handful of other locations. In World War II even the most remote and strategically protected countries were not immune to attack. Of the major belligerents in the war, only the US did not suffer any domestic losses as a result of action on the home front.

People can be forgiven for assuming that the principle victims of World War II were the Jews, who were slaughtered in their millions by the Germans in those years. There are no words to describe the horror of genocide, nor the systematic and cold-hearted way in which the Germans carried out the task. While the key figures in the Nazi regime paid for their decisions and their politics, either at Nuremberg or by their own hands, there were thousands of others who left indelible scars, not just on the victims themselves and their families, but their ancestors several generations removed.

The war's lasting legacy is the fact that after several generations, those across the world who are far too young to remember any of the direct consequences of World War II, remain fascinated and engaged by the collective memory of it.

BIBLIOGRAPHY

Ambrose, Stephen E., *D-Day, June 6 1944 – The Battle for the Normandy Beaches*, Pocket Books, 2002

Atkinson, Rick, *An Army at Dawn: The War in North Africa 1942–1943*, Little, Brown, 2003

Ball, S. J., *The Cold War: An International History, 1947–1991*, London, 1998

Banks, A., *A Military Atlas of the First World War*, London, 1975

Beevor, Antony, *Stalingrad*, Penguin, 1999

Beevor, Antony, *The Fall of Berlin 1945*, Penguin, 2003

Bruce, George, *Collins Dictionary of Wars*, London, 1995

Bullock, Alan, *Hitler and Stalin: Parallel Lives*, Fontana Press, 1998

Calvocoressi, Peter, *World Politics Since 1945*, New York, 1991

Calvocoressi, Peter, et al, *The Penguin History of the Second World War*, Penguin, 2003

Chandler, David, *The Dictionary of Battles*, London, 1987

Churchill, Winston, *The Second World War*, Pimlico, 2002

Cross, F. L., *The Oxford Dictionary of the Christian Church*, Oxford University Press, Oxford, 1978

Fussell, P., *The Great War and Modern Memory*, London, 1975

Gardiner, Judith, *The History Today Who's Who in British History*, Collins and Brown, London, 2000

Gilbert, Martin, *First World War*, HarperCollins, London, 1994

Gilbert, Martin, *Second World War*, London, 1989

Gilbert, Martin, *The Holocaust*, HarperCollins, 1987

Gilbert, Martin, *Churchill: A Life*, Pimlico, 2000

Haigh, Christopher (ed.), *The Cambridge Historical Encyclopedia of Great Britain and Ireland*, Cambridge, 1996

Hart, L., *The History of the Second World War*, London, 1970

Hobsbawn, E. J., *The Age of Extremes, 1919–1991*, London, 1994

Holland, James, *Fortress Malta: An Island Under Siege 1940–1943*, Orion, 2003

Jackson, Julian, *France: The Dark Years, 1940–1944*, Oxford University Press, 2003

Jackson, Julian, *The Fall of France: The Nazi Invasion of 1940*, Oxford University Press, 2003

Kershaw, Ian, *Hitler 1936–1945*, Penguin, 2001

Layton, Geoff, *Germany: The Third Reich 1933–45*, Hodder and Stoughton, 2000

Messenger, Charles, *The Century of Warfare: Worldwide Conflict from 1900 to the Present Day*, London, 1995

Morgan, Kenneth O. (ed.), *The Oxford Illustrated History of Britain*, Oxford, 1997

Morillo, S., *Warfare Under the Anglo-Norman Kings, 1066–1135*, Woodbridge, 1994

Pollard, A. J., *The Wars of the Roses*, London, 1988

Pope, R. (ed.), *Atlas of British Social and Economic History Since c. 1700*, London, 1990

Radway, R., *Britain, 1900–1951*, London, 1997

Roseman, Mark, *The Villa, The Lake, The Meeting: Wannsee and the Final Solution*, Penguin, 2003

Ryan, Cornelius, *A Bridge Too Far*, Wordsworth Editions, 1999

Sweeman, John, et al, *The Dambusters*, Time Warner, 2003

Taylor, A. J. P., *English History, 1914–1945*, Oxford, 1965

Taylor, A. J. P., *From the Boer War to the Cold War*, London, 1995

Trotter, William R., *The Winter War: The Russo-Finnish War of 1939–40*, Aurum Books, 2002

Tucker, S. C., *The Great War*, London, 1998

Weintraub, Stanley, *Long Day's Journey Into War*: December 7 1941, Lyons Press, 2001

Young, John, W., *Britain and the World in the Twentieth Century*, London, 1997

Young, Peter (ed), *The Cassell Atlas of the Second World War*, Cassell, 1999

WEB SITES

www.bbc.co.uk/history/war/wwtwo/

www.ibiblio.org/hyperwar/

www.codesandciphers.org.uk/

www.spartacus.schoolnet.co.uk/2ww/

historyplace.com/worldwar2/

AUTHORS

Jon Sutherland is a full-time writer and author of over eighty books. His most recent titles include *Unsolved Victorian Murders, African Americans At War, Elite Forces of World War Two*. Jon is currently working on a series of educational reference glossaries for Business Studies graduates, a Zulu military history book and a series of interactive war books. Jon lives in Suffolk with his partner Diane Canwell and two children.

Diane Canwell is also a full-time writer and author of over fifty books. Her most recent titles include *Women Who Shocked The Nation, Leisure and Tourism GCSE* and *Vikings*. Diane is also working on a series of glossary texts in Business related topics, several Business Administration books and a major history book called *Women in the American Civil War*. Diane lives in Suffolk with her partner Jon Sutherland.

INTRODUCTION
Paul Cornish has spent the past fourteen years working as a curator at the Imperial War Museum in London, managing many of their collections and specializing in firearms and edged weapons. He has contributed to a number of reference works on military subjects and has written numerous articles, on subjects as diverse as the Chinese Nationalist army, General Vlasov, and the weapons of the Special Operations Executive. He is currently engaged in a study of the material culture of twentieth-century conflict.

PICTURE CREDITS

INDEX